BETTER HOMES AND GARDENS®

COOKING FOR TODAY

HOT & SPICY

BETTER HOMES AND GARDENS® BOOKS
Des Moines

BETTER HOMES AND GARDENS® BOOKS
An Imprint of Meredith® Books

HOT & SPICY
Editors: Lisa Mannes, Mary Major Williams
Writer: Linda Foley Woodrum
Associate Art Director: Tom Wegner
Electronic Production Coordinator: Paula Forest
Test Kitchen Product Supervisors: Diana Nolin, Colleen Weeden
Food Stylists: Lynn Blanchard, Janet Pittman, Jennifer Peterson
Photographers: Mike Dieter, Scott Little
Production Manager: Douglas Johnston

Vice President and Editorial Director: Elizabeth P. Rice
Executive Editor: Kay Sanders
Art Director: Ernest Shelton
Managing Editor: Christopher Cavanaugh
Test Kitchen Director: Sharon Stilwell

President, Book Group: Joseph J. Ward
Vice President, Retail Marketing: Jamie L. Martin
Vice President, Direct Marketing: Timothy Jarrell

On the cover: Red Lentil Tostadas (see recipe, page 130)

Meredith Corporation
Chairman of the Executive Committee: E. T. Meredith III
Chairman of the Board and Chief Executive Officer: Jack D. Rehm
President and Chief Operating Officer: William T. Kerr

WE CARE!

All of us at Better Homes and Gardens® Books are dedicated to providing you with the information and ideas you need to create delicious foods. We welcome your comments and suggestions. Write to us at: Better Homes and Gardens® Books, Cookbook Editorial Department, RW-240, 1716 Locust St., Des Moines, IA 50309-3023

If you would like to order additional copies of any of our books, call 1-800-678-2803 or check with your local bookstore.

Our seal assures you that every recipe in *Hot & Spicy* has been tested in the Better Homes and Gardens® Test Kitchen. This means that each recipe is practical and reliable, and meets our high standards of taste appeal. We guarantee your satisfaction with this book for as long as you own it.

W hen it comes to seasoning food, some like it hot! If you fit that category, then you'll welcome the fiery feasts that are featured in this book. What makes food hot and spicy? Take your pick—searing chili peppers, pungent peppercorns, aromatic horseradish, tingling ginger, and mouth-burning mustard. These seasonings not only provide heat but enliven foods with new flavors, textures, and colors.

You'll have no problem warming up to the recipes in this book, such as Gunpowder Guacamole, Warm Thai Beef Salad, Red Chili Chicken with Goat Cheese, and Shrimp with Serranos. How hot are the recipes? Since each person has a different level of heat tolerance, we rated the recipes either hot, hotter, or hottest. If your passion for heat is new, you may want to start off with the recipe labeled "hot." If you have a well-tempered tongue, then go ahead and try every recipe labeled "hottest." The "hotter" recipes are for those who fall somewhere in between. No matter what your preference, you'll discover the joy of heat with these recipes.

CONTENTS

BUYING AND STORING FRESH CHILI PEPPERS

When buying fresh chili peppers, choose ones that are firm and heavy for their size. The skin should be free of blemishes, smooth, and shiny. Give them a sniff and choose ones that have a fresh, clean smell. Once you get them home, wash the chili peppers, dry them, wrap them in paper towels, and store them in your refrigerator. They will stay fresh, when stored this way, for 2 to 3 weeks. Do not store chili peppers in plastic bags because moisture will accumulate, causing them to spoil quicker. Avoid leaving them uncovered on your counter because they will dry out and lose flavor and texture.

BUYING AND STORING DRIED CHILI PEPPERS

When buying dried chili peppers, go for the ones that are clean, unbroken, and have a uniform color that is deep or brilliant. Good quality dried chilies have some flexibility to them and should not be brittle. They should have a pleasant aroma similar to fresh spices. Avoid peppers that have spots on them which can mean they have been improperly stored or harbor disease. Store dried chili peppers in an airtight container in a cool, dry place. For best flavor and texture, use within 6 months.

HANDLE WITH CARE

Exercise caution when working with chili peppers because they contain volatile oils that can burn your skin and eyes. Your best defense, if your skin is very sensitive to the oils, is to wear plastic or rubber gloves as you work with the chili peppers. If you are less sensitive, use your bare hands but be sure to wash your hands and fingernails well with soap and water when you are done.

WHY ARE CHILI PEPPERS HOT?

The fiery sensation in your mouth when eating chili peppers is caused by a potent chemical called capsaicin, which can survive cooking and freezing. An extremely hot chili pepper, such as habanero, contains a greater amount of capsaicin than a milder chili pepper, such as poblano. Most of the heat is contained in the membranes, seeds, and ribs of the chili pepper. In general, small chili peppers are hotter than large chili peppers because the smaller ones have a higher proportion of membranes and seeds than the larger peppers. To turn down the heat of any chili pepper, remove the membranes and seeds.

PUTTING OUT THE FIRE

For tender tongues that get scorched after eating something hot and spicy (particularly chili peppers), there is easy relief. Reach for dairy products such as milk, sour cream, yogurt, or ice cream. If those aren't handy, then eat something starchy like bread or rice which will neutralize the alkaloids in chili peppers, reducing the burn a little bit. Avoid drinking alcohol or carbonated beverages since they tend to make the food seem hotter.

HOT CHILI PEPPER PUREE

For a fiery addition to soups, stews, sauces, pasta, or salad dressings, try this easy chili pepper puree.

Rinse 4 dried *chipotle chili peppers.* Cut peppers open and discard stems and seeds. Place peppers in a bowl. Pour 1 cup *boiling water* over peppers. Let stand for 20 to 30 minutes or till softened. *Do not* drain.

Transfer chili pepper mixture to a food processor bowl or blender container. Cover and process or blend till smooth. (Do not breathe the fumes.) Cover and chill to store. Makes about 1 cup.

Ancho Chili Pepper Puree: For a milder version, prepare Hot Chili Pepper Puree as directed above, *except* substitute 2 *ancho chili peppers* for the chipotle chili peppers.

HOMEMADE CURRY POWDER

Here's a sure-fire way to guarantee the freshest curry powder....make your own! It's easy.

In a blender container or electric spice mill place 4½ teaspoons ground *coriander* or 1 tablespoon coriander seed, 2 teaspoons ground *turmeric,* 1½ teaspoons *cumin seed,* 1½ teaspoons *crushed red pepper,* 1 teaspoon *whole black peppercorns,* ½ teaspoon whole *cardamom seed* (without pods), 1-inch broken stick *cinnamon,* ¼ teaspoon whole *cloves,* and ¼ teaspoon ground *ginger.* Cover and grind to a fine powder (this may take 2 to 3 minutes).

Store curry powder in an airtight container in a cool, dry place. Makes about ¼ cup.

CHILI PEPPERS

Chili peppers range in flavor from mild to fiery. Refer to the information on these pages when selecting different varieties for cooking.

Poblano: This dark green or ripe red chili pepper varies in strength between medium and hot (the red is slightly sweeter than the green). It is one of the most popular chili peppers in Mexico and typically eaten cooked or roasted, not raw. This is the chili pepper of choice when making chili rellenos, but also good in sauces and chili.

Ancho: This is a dried poblano chili pepper and used extensively in Mexican cooking. The ancho (which means "wide" in Spanish) is the sweetest of the dried peppers with mild fruit flavors and tones of coffee, plums, and raisins. It is most commonly used in mole sauces.

De Arbol: This brick-red elongated pepper is closely related to the cayenne pepper. De arbol peppers have a searing heat on the tip of the tongue and smokey, grassy tones. Use it dried or in its powdered form in sauces and soups.

Cascabel: This reddish brown, smooth chili pepper has a medium hotness with subtle smokey and nutty flavors. The heat from this pepper is noticeable in the back of the throat. Try it in sauces, soups, and stews.

Mulato: This pepper is a type of dried poblano chili pepper (like the ancho). It has a smokier flavor than the ancho pepper without the lingering taste. Try it in soups, stews, and sauces.

Serrano: This small chili pepper is green or bright red (when fully ripe) with a clean biting heat and pleasant acidity. It is the hottest chili pepper commonly available in the United States. Use it in salsas, sauces, marinades, and salads.

Habanero: This chili pepper, also called Scotch Bonnet, ranges in color from dark green, to orange to orange red and to red when fully ripe. Habanero (meaning "from Havana") is one of the hottest chili peppers grown in the world. It is estimated that this fiery pepper is 30 to 50 times hotter than a jalepeño pepper. Try it sparingly in salsas and marinades.

Anaheim: Also called California or long green or long red chili pepper. This mild pepper comes in green and red, with the red having more sweetness. Anaheim chili peppers are used in cooking for chili rellenos, stews, and sauces.

Jalepeño: This chili pepper, probably the best known in the United States, ranges from dark green to bright red (when it is fully ripe). The red version is sweeter than the green, yet both types provide a medium hotness. Use it in almost any recipe for spiciness such as salsas, dips, marinades, salads, sauces, breads, and nachos.

Chipotle: This is a dried, smoked jalepeño pepper with a medium to hot rating and a smokey, chocolate flavor. Used extensively in Mexican and Southwest cooking, it is also available canned in adobo sauce.

GUNPOWDER GUACAMOLE

Heat rating: Hot
Load this chunky dip on a crisp tortilla chip and fire away!

2 medium avocados, seeded, peeled, and cut up
1 tablespoon lime juice
1 medium red sweet pepper, roasted and chopped* or ½ cup chopped purchased roasted red pepper
3 green onions, finely chopped
1 to 2 tablespoons chopped jalapeño or serrano chili peppers
¼ teaspoon salt
¼ teaspoon ground black pepper
⅛ teaspoon ground red pepper
Tortilla chips

In a medium mixing bowl combine avocados and lime juice. Using a potato masher, coarsely mash avocado mixture (mixture should be slightly lumpy).

Stir roasted sweet pepper, green onions, jalapeño or serrano peppers, salt, black pepper, and red pepper into avocado mixture. Cover and chill till serving time. Serve with tortilla chips. Makes about 1⅔ cups.

*Note: To roast sweet red pepper, halve pepper and remove stem, membrane, and seeds. Place pepper, cut side down, on a foil-lined baking sheet. Bake in a 425° oven for 20 to 25 minutes or till skin is bubbly and black. Place pepper in a clean brown paper bag; seal and let stand for 20 to 30 minutes or till cool enough to handle. Pull the skin off gently and discard.

Nutrition facts per serving: 26 calories, 2 g total fat (0 g saturated fat), 0 mg cholesterol, 21 mg sodium, 2 g carbohydrate, 1 g fiber, 0 g protein.
Daily Value: 3% vitamin A, 12% vitamin C, 0% calcium, 1% iron.

GOAT CHEESE AND PEPPER-STUFFED FLATBREAD

Heat rating: Hot

If making yeast bread doesn't fit into your busy schedule, you can still enjoy this spicy appetizer by using two 1-pound loaves of frozen bread dough, thawed.

4¼ to 4¾ cups all-purpose flour
  2 tablespoons sugar
  1 package active dry yeast
  ½ teaspoon salt
  ¼ teaspoon cracked black pepper
1½ cups warm water (120° to 130°)
  1 egg, slightly beaten
  2 dried ancho, mulato, or pasilla chili peppers or combination of two varieties
  6 to 8 ounces chèvre (goat cheese)
  ⅓ cup chopped green onions or shallots
     Milk
     Cracked black pepper
     Green onion brushes (optional)

For dough, in a large mixing bowl stir together *2 cups* of the flour, sugar, yeast, salt, and *¼ teaspoon* cracked black pepper. Add water and egg. Beat with an electric mixer on low speed for 30 seconds, scraping the sides of the bowl constantly. Beat on high speed for 3 minutes. Stir in as much flour as you can.

On a lightly floured surface, knead in enough of the remaining flour to make a moderately soft dough that is smooth and elastic (6 to 8 minutes total). Shape into a ball. Place in a lightly greased bowl and turn once to grease surface. Cover and let rise in a warm place till double in size (about 1 hour).

Meanwhile, wash dried chili peppers in cold water; remove stems and seeds. Place in a bowl of boiling water and soak for 1 hour. Drain well. Chop drained peppers.

Punch down dough. Divide in half. Cover and let rest 10 minutes. Lightly oil a 12- or 13-inch round pizza pan. On a lightly floured surface roll half of the dough into a ¼-inch thick round. Transfer to prepared pan. Crumble or spoon goat cheese over dough. Sprinkle with chili peppers and green onions. Roll out remaining dough to a ¼-inch thick round. Place over goat cheese mixture. Press edges to seal. Using tines of a fork, press dough down to flatten slightly. Brush top with milk and sprinkle with additional cracked black pepper.

Bake in a 400° oven about 20 minutes or till top is light brown and bread is cooked through. Cool slightly. Serve warm or at room temperature. Makes 8 appetizer servings.

Nutrition facts per serving: 323 calories, 7g total fat (3 g saturated fat), 46 mg cholesterol, 269 mg sodium, 52 g carbohydrate, 2 g fiber, 12 g protein.
Daily Value: 12% vitamin A, 19% vitamin C, 3% calcium, 22% iron.

FRIED DEVILED BRIE

Heat rating: Hot

For best results, choose a wheel of Brie that's fairly firm when you squeeze it gently.

1   8-ounce round Brie or Camembert
      cheese, chilled
2   tablespoons all-purpose flour
2   teaspoons dry mustard
1   egg
2   tablespoons milk
½   cup fine dry bread crumbs
¼   teaspoon ground red pepper
¼   teaspoon ground black pepper
      Oil for deep-fat frying
      Fresh herbs
½   cup jalapeño or other pepper jelly,
      warmed

Cut cheese into 8 wedges. Set aside. On a piece of waxed paper, a small plate, or a small mixing bowl stir together flour and mustard. In another small mixing bowl stir together egg and milk. In another small mixing bowl stir together bread crumbs, red pepper, and black pepper.

Coat each piece of cheese in flour mixture. Dip into egg mixture and coat with bread crumb mixture. Dip again into egg mixture and then into bread crumb mixture.

Deep-fry coated cheese wedges in hot oil (365°) for 30 to 60 seconds or till golden brown. Drain on paper towels. Garnish with fresh herbs and serve warm with jelly. Makes 8 appetizer servings.

Nutrition facts per serving: 220 calories, 12 g total fat (6 g saturated fat), 55 mg cholesterol, 239 mg sodium, 19 g carbohydrate, 0 g fiber, 8 g protein.
Daily Value: *7% vitamin A, 0% vitamin C, 5% calcium, 4% iron.*

MINI BALLS OF FIRE

Heat rating: Hottest

Temper these fire-breathing meatballs with a cool chutney for dipping. The heat comes from habanero chili peppers, also called Scotch Bonnet peppers, which are the hottest peppers in the world. If you can't locate them, substitute another hot pepper such as tepin or tabasco.

1	beaten egg
¼	cup fine dry bread crumbs
¼	cup milk
2	tablespoons snipped fresh mint or cilantro
1½	teaspoons finely chopped habanero chili pepper
½	teaspoon salt
½	teaspoon ground cinnamon
½	teaspoon ground ginger
¼	teaspoon ground nutmeg
¼	teaspoon ground black pepper
⅛	teaspoon ground cloves
1	pound ground lamb or beef
1	cup chutney

In a large mixing bowl stir together egg, bread crumbs, milk, mint or cilantro, chili pepper, salt, cinnamon, ginger, nutmeg, black pepper, and cloves. Add lamb or beef; mix well.

Shape meat mixture into 1-inch meatballs. Place in a 15x10x1-inch baking pan. Bake in a 350° oven for 15 to 20 minutes or till no longer pink. Drain on paper towels. Serve warm with chutney. Makes 48 meatball appetizers.

Nutrition facts per meatball: 36 calories, 1 g total fat (1 g saturated fat), 11 mg cholesterol, 35 mg sodium, 4 g carbohydrate, 0 g fiber, 2 g protein.
Daily Value: 0% vitamin A, 1% vitamin C, 0% calcium, 1% iron.

OYSTERS SALSAFELLER

Heat rating: Hot

Make this spicy version of Oysters Rockefeller as hot as your tongue can take by choosing the salsa of your choice.

2 cups chopped fresh spinach
¼ cup chopped shallots or onion
2 cloves garlic, minced
1 cup salsa
24 oysters in shells
¼ cup fine dry bread crumbs
¼ teaspoon ground cumin
1 tablespoon margarine or
   butter, melted

In a saucepan cook spinach, shallots or onions, and garlic in one tablespoon boiling water for 3 to 5 minutes or till tender. Drain; press out excess moisture. Stir in salsa.

Thoroughly wash oysters. Open shells with an oyster knife or other blunt-tipped knife. Remove oysters and dry. Discard flat top shells. Wash bottom shells. Place each oyster in a bottom shell.

Spoon spinach-salsa mixture over oysters. Combine bread crumbs and cumin. Toss with melted margarine. Sprinkle over oysters.

Line a shallow baking pan with rock salt to about ½-inch depth. (Or, use crumpled foil to keep shells from tipping over.) Arrange oysters on top. Bake in a 425° oven for 10 to 12 minutes or till edges of oysters begin to curl. Makes 6 to 8 appetizer servings.

Nutrition facts per serving: 230 calories, 8 g total fat (1 g saturated fat), 0 mg cholesterol, 431 mg sodium, 19 g carbohydrate, 1 g fiber, 21 g protein.
Daily Value: 40% vitamin A, 26% vitamin C, 5% calcium, 72% iron.

CROSTINI

Heat rating: Hot

These crisp slices of French bread are topped with a piquant tomato, olive, and chili pepper mixture. Be sure to drain the topping well to prevent the bread from becoming soggy.

2   medium ripe tomatoes, peeled, seeded, and chopped (1 cup)
4   Calamata olives, pitted and chopped or pitted ripe olives, chopped
¼   cup finely chopped red onion
1   canned anchovy fillet, drained, patted dry, and chopped (optional)
1   tablespoon balsamic or red wine vinegar
1   tablespoon finely chopped poblano chili pepper
1   large clove garlic, minced
1   8-ounce loaf baguette-style French bread
5   ounces mozzarella cheese, thinly sliced

In a medium mixing bowl stir together tomatoes, olives, onion, anchovy (if desired), vinegar, chili pepper, and garlic. Let stand at room temperature for 20 to 30 minutes.

Meanwhile, bias-slice the bread into ½-inch-thick slices. Place bread slices on a baking sheet.

Bake bread in a 350° oven about 5 minutes or till light brown. Turn bread over and bake 5 minutes more.

Evenly distribute mozzarella cheese slices over toasted bread. Drain tomato and olive mixture. Top slices with a spoonful of tomato and olive mixture.

Return bread slices to oven and bake for 5 minutes more or till cheese melts and tomato and olive mixture is heated through. Makes about 20 crostini.

Nutrition facts per crostini: 54 calories, 2 g total fat (1 g saturated fat), 4 mg cholesterol, 114 mg sodium, 7 g carbohydrate, 0 g fiber, 3 g protein.
Daily Value: *2% vitamin A, 6% vitamin C, 4% calcium, 2% iron.*

WOW! WINGS

Heat rating: Hottest

Whew! These wings are really hot but the cool dipping sauce helps tame the flame.

12 chicken wings (about 2 pounds)
    Oil for deep-fat frying
 3 tablespoons margarine or butter
 1 2-ounce bottle hot pepper
        sauce (¼ cup)
 ½ cup dairy sour cream
 ¼ cup mayonnaise or salad dressing
 2 tablespoons snipped fresh basil
 2 tablespoons snipped fresh parsley
 1 tablespoon milk
    Fresh basil sprig (optional)

Cut off and discard tips of chicken wings. Cut wing at joints to form 24 pieces. Rinse pieces and pat dry. Fry wing pieces, a few at a time, in deep hot oil (375°) for 8 to 10 minutes or till golden brown and no longer pink. Drain on paper towels. Keep pieces warm in a 300° oven while frying remaining pieces. Transfer wings to a serving dish.

In a saucepan melt margarine or butter. Stir in hot pepper sauce. Pour over wings, turning wings to coat.

For dipping sauce, in a small mixing bowl stir together sour cream, mayonnaise or salad dressing, basil, parsley, and milk. Serve wings with dipping sauce. Garnish sauce with fresh basil, if desired. Makes 8 to 12 appetizer servings.

Nutrition facts per serving: 331 calories, 30 g total fat (8 g saturated fat), 51 mg cholesterol, 166 mg sodium, 1 g carbohydrate, 0 g fiber, 14 g protein.
***Daily Value:** 12% vitamin A, 10% vitamin C, 2% calcium, 5% iron.*

STUFFED JALAPEÑOS

Heat rating: Hottest

This recipe works equally well with Anaheim chili peppers. For best results, choose Anaheim peppers that are long and skinny.

4 ounces soft-style cream cheese
2 tablespoons finely chopped
      green onion
2 tablespoons chopped pimiento,
      drained
1 clove garlic, minced
12 jalapeño chili peppers or 2 to 3
      Anaheim chili peppers, halved
      lengthwise and seeded

In a small mixing bowl stir together cream cheese, green onion, pimiento, and garlic. Spoon mixture into jalapeño or Anaheim pepper halves. Cover and chill till serving time.

Before serving Anaheim stuffed peppers, cut into 2-inch bite-size pieces. Makes about 12 appetizer servings.

Nutrition facts per serving: 42 calories, 3 g total fat (2 g saturated fat), 10 mg cholesterol, 35 mg sodium, 2 g carbohydrate, 0 g fiber, 1 g protein.
Daily Value: 3% vitamin A, 79% vitamin C, 0% calcium, 1% iron.

WARM THAI BEEF SALAD

Heat rating: Hotter

Be sure to use hot bean paste, not a milder bean sauce, to get the maximum heat from this main dish salad.
Look for bean paste at large supermarkets, specialty food stores, or Asian markets.

12   ounces flank steak, trimmed of fat
¼   cup plum sauce
2   tablespoons red wine vinegar
1   tablespoon water
1   to 2 teaspoons hot bean paste
¼   to ½ teaspoon crushed red pepper
4   cups torn mixed greens such as curly
       endive, spinach, arugula, radicchio,
       watercress, and/or leaf lettuce
1   11-ounce can mandarin oranges,
       drained
2   tablespoons cooking oil
3   serrano chili peppers, seeded and
       finely chopped
1   red sweet pepper, cut into strips
       (1 cup)
1   yellow sweet pepper, cut into strips
       (1 cup)
1   clove garlic, minced

Partially freeze meat and cut across the grain into thin strips. In a small mixing bowl stir together plum sauce, vinegar, water, hot bean paste, and red pepper; set aside.

On four individual serving plates arrange mixed greens and drained oranges; set aside.

In a wok or large skillet heat *1 tablespoon* of the oil over medium-high heat. Add chili peppers, sweet peppers, and garlic to hot skillet. Cook and stir for 3 to 4 minutes or till sweet peppers are crisp-tender. Remove peppers from skillet.

Heat remaining oil in wok or skillet. Add beef to hot oil. Cook and stir for 2 to 3 minutes or till desired doneness. Add plum sauce mixture to skillet. Stir to coat meat. Return peppers to wok or skillet. Cook and stir for 2 minutes or till heated through.

Spoon meat mixture over mixed greens on plates. Serve warm. Makes 4 servings.

Nutrition facts per serving: 283 calories, 17 g total fat (4 g saturated fat), 40 mg cholesterol, 177 mg sodium, 18 g carbohydrate, 2 g fiber, 21 g protein.
Daily Value: 52% vitamin A, 204% vitamin C, 5% calcium, 24% iron.

GRILLED SOUTHWEST STEAK

Heat rating: Hot

Balance the spiciness by serving a cooling fruit salsa with the grilled steak. Simply toss together 1 cup chopped fresh peaches or apricots, ¼ cup chopped green or red sweet pepper, 2 tablespoons sliced green onion, 1 tablespoon honey, and 1 tablespoon lime juice.

⅓ **cup cooking oil**
⅓ **cup lime juice**
3 **jalapeño chili peppers, chopped**
3 **shallots, chopped**
2 **cloves garlic, minced**
2 **tablespoons snipped fresh cilantro**
¼ **teaspoon salt**
1 **pound beef round steak, cut**
     1 inch thick

For marinade, in a small mixing bowl stir together oil, lime juice, chili peppers, shallots, garlic, cilantro, and salt.

Place steak in a plastic bag. Set the bag in a deep bowl. Pour marinade over steak. Close bag tightly and turn to coat steaks. Marinate in the refrigerator for 6 hours or overnight, turning bag occasionally.

Drain steak, reserving marinade. Grill steak, on an uncovered grill, directly over medium coals. For rare doneness, grill for 24 to 26 minutes and for medium doneness, grill for 28 to 30 minutes or till done, turning the steaks over halfway through the grilling time. Brush with reserved marinade occasionally during grilling. Do not brush with marinade the last 5 minutes of grilling. Makes 4 servings.

Nutrition facts per serving: 229 calories, 12 g total fat (3 g saturated fat), 72 mg cholesterol, 186 mg sodium, 1 g carbohydrate, 0 g fiber, 27 g protein.
Daily Value: 2% vitamin A, 18% vitamin C, 0% calcium, 16% iron.

BEEF AND CHIPOTLE PINWHEELS

Heat rating: Hot

If using dried chipotle peppers instead of canned, use 1 or 2 and soften them in boiling water or beef broth for 10 minutes.

3	canned chipotle chili peppers, drained
2	tablespoons beef broth
2	cloves garlic
1	1- to 1½-pound beef flank steak
½	teaspoon salt
¼	teaspoon ground black pepper
¼	cup snipped fresh chives
1	tablespoon margarine or butter
1	tablespoon all-purpose flour
1	tablespoon Dijon-style mustard
½	cup milk
½	cup beef broth
1	tablespoon snipped fresh chives

In a blender container or food processor combine chili peppers, *2 tablespoons* broth, and garlic. Cover and blend or process till smooth. Set aside.

Score steak by making shallow cuts at 1-inch intervals diagonally across the steak in a diamond pattern. Repeat on second side of meat. Using a meat mallet, pound the steak into a 12x8-inch rectangle, working from the center out to the edges. Sprinkle with salt and black pepper.

Spread chili pepper mixture over meat. Sprinkle with *¼ cup* chives. Starting from the narrow end, roll up steak, jelly-roll style. Skewer with wooden toothpicks at 1-inch intervals. Cut between toothpicks into eight 1-inch slices.

Place slices, cut side down, on the unheated rack of a broiler pan. Broil 3 inches from the heat for 6 minutes. Turn and broil till desired doneness, allowing 6 to 8 minutes more for medium. Remove wooden toothpicks.

Meanwhile, for sauce, in a small saucepan melt margarine or butter. Stir in flour and mustard. Add milk and *½ cup* broth. Cook and stir over medium heat till thickened and bubbly. Cook and stir 1 minute more. Stir in *1 tablespoon* chives. Serve with meat. Makes 4 servings.

Nutrition facts per serving: 225 calories, 12 g total fat (4 g saturated fat), 55 mg cholesterol, 730 mg sodium, 5 g carbohydrate, 0 g fiber, 24 g protein.
Daily Value: 7% vitamin A, 18% vitamin C, 4% calcium, 16% iron.

SPICY GRILLED BRISKET

Heat rating: Hotter

If you don't have a hungry crowd to feed, then plan on great sandwiches all week long. Thinly slice any leftover meat and serve on Kaiser rolls with lettuce and horseradish sauce.

1½ **pounds mesquite wood chunks**
1 **5- to 6-pound fresh beef brisket**
3 **cloves garlic, cut into slivers**
2 **tablespoons cooking oil**
2 **tablespoons coarse or kosher salt**
2 **tablespoons paprika**
1 **tablespoon ground black pepper**
1 **teaspoon ground red pepper**
1 **teaspoon dried thyme, crushed**
Sweet and Hot Barbecue Sauce
(see recipe, page 140) or bottled
barbecue sauce

At least one hour before grilling, soak wood chunks in enough water to cover.

Trim fat from brisket. Make several slits in both surfaces of the brisket and poke a sliver of garlic into each slit. Brush the brisket with oil. In a small mixing bowl stir together salt, paprika, black pepper, red pepper, and thyme. Rub pepper mixture over all sides of the meat.

Drain wood chunks. In a covered grill arrange preheated coals around a drip pan; test for medium-low heat above pan. Place about *half* of the drained wood chunks on top of the preheated coals.

Place brisket on grill rack, fat side up, over drip pan but not over coals. Lower grill hood. Grill for 2½ to 3 hours or till tender, adding more dampened wood chunks and charcoal briquettes, if necessary.

Meanwhile, prepare sauce or warm bottled sauce in a small saucepan over low heat. To serve, let meat stand 10 minutes. Slice meat across the grain. Serve with barbecue sauce. Makes 15 servings.

Nutrition facts per serving: 243 calories, 11 g total fat (3 g saturated fat), 76 g cholesterol, 1,343 mg sodium, 11 g carbohydrate, 0 g fiber, 25 g protein.
Daily Value: 9% vitamin A, 2% vitamin C, 1% calcium, 18% iron.

TAMALE PIE

Heat rating: Hot

Cocoa powder in a main dish pie? Yep! It helps blend the flavors of the other seasonings and gives this entrée a robust background flavor. Although the ingredient list is long, this ground meat pie is a cinch to make.

1¼ cups cold water
½ cup yellow cornmeal
1 teaspoon ground cumin
½ teaspoon paprika
¼ teaspoon salt
¼ teaspoon ground black pepper
2 teaspoons margarine or butter
1 pound lean ground beef
1 cup chopped onion
1 medium green sweet pepper,
     chopped (¾ cup)
2 cloves garlic, minced
1 15-ounce can tomato sauce
1 10-ounce package frozen whole kernel
     corn, thawed
1 tablespoon yellow cornmeal
1 tablespoon chili powder
1 tablespoon ground cumin
2 teaspoons unsweetened cocoa powder
½ teaspoon ground allspice
½ to 1 teaspoon bottled hot
     pepper sauce
¼ teaspoon ground black pepper
½ cup shredded sharp cheddar cheese
     (2 ounces)

In a small saucepan combine water, *½ cup* cornmeal, *1 teaspoon* cumin, paprika, salt, and *¼ teaspoon* black pepper. Bring just to boiling; reduce heat. Stir in margarine or butter. Cook, uncovered, over low heat for 10 minutes, stirring often. Remove from heat. Spread mixture on waxed paper into an 8-inch square. Chill while preparing meat mixture.

In a large skillet cook beef, onion, sweet pepper, and garlic over medium heat till meat is brown and onion is tender. Drain off fat. Stir in tomato sauce, corn, *1 tablespoon* cornmeal, chili powder, *1 tablespoon* cumin, cocoa powder, allspice, hot pepper sauce, and *¼ teaspoon* black pepper. Bring to boiling; reduce heat. Simmer, uncovered, for 5 minutes.

Spoon meat mixture into a 2-quart rectangular baking dish. Cut cornmeal mixture into desired shapes, piecing together scraps, if necessary. Place on top of meat mixture.

Bake, uncovered, in a 375° oven about 30 minutes or till bubbly and cornmeal topping is light brown. Remove from oven and immediately sprinkle with cheese. Let stand 2 to 3 minutes till cheese melts. Makes 6 servings.

Nutrition facts per serving: 327 calories, 14 g total fat (6 g saturated fat), 57 mg cholesterol, 678 mg sodium, 31 g carbohydrate, 4 g fiber, 21 g protein.
Daily Value: 19% vitamin A, 29% vitamin C, 9% calcium, 22% iron.

TEXAS CHILI

Heat rating: Hottest

For the crushed small hot dried chili peppers, use cayenne, de arbol, pequin, serrano seco, or tepin. Use 12 to 50 peppers (depending on their size) to get 1 to 2 tablespoons crushed.

3   dried ancho chili peppers, seeded

1   to 2 tablespoons crushed small hot dried chili peppers or 1 to 2 tablespoons crushed red pepper

2½ pounds beef round steak, cut into ½-inch cubes

2   tablespoons cooking oil

1   medium onion, chopped (½ cup)

4   cloves garlic, minced

2   teaspoons ground cumin

6   medium tomatoes, peeled, seeded, and coarsely chopped (3 cups)

1   10½-ounce can condensed beef broth

1⅓ cups water

½   teaspoon dried oregano, crushed

    Cooked red kidney beans (optional)

    Sliced pickled peppers (optional)

Cut chili peppers into small pieces. Place all the peppers in a blender container or food processor bowl. Cover and blend or process till ground. Set aside.

In a Dutch oven brown *half* of the meat in hot oil. With a slotted spoon, remove meat from saucepan; set aside. Add remaining meat, onion, garlic, cumin, and the ground chili peppers. Cook till meat is brown.

Return all of the meat to the Dutch oven. Stir in tomatoes, broth, water, and oregano. Bring to boiling; reduce heat. Simmer, uncovered, for 1¼ to 1½ hours or till meat is tender, stirring occasionally Serve with cooked kidney beans, if desired. Garnish each serving with pickled peppers, if desired. Makes 6 servings.

Nutrition facts per serving: 367 calories, 14 g total fat (4 g saturated fat), 120 mg cholesterol, 455 mg sodium, 10 g carbohydrate, 3 g fiber, 48 g protein.
Daily Value: 27% vitamin A, 41% vitamin C, 4% calcium, 42% iron.

STEAK AU POIVRE

Heat rating: Hotter

This classic French beef masterpiece (pronounced o PWAV-rah) gets its spiciness from lots of cracked black pepper. Try it with other cuts of beef, such as beef rib eye or tenderloin steaks.

4 beef top loin steaks, cut 1 inch thick (about 2 pounds)
1 tablespoon cracked black pepper
2 tablespoons margarine or butter
    Salt
¼ cup brandy
¼ cup beef broth
¼ cup whipping cream
4 teaspoons Dijon-style mustard
1 tablespoon green peppercorns in brine, drained

Slash the fat edge of the steaks at 1-inch intervals. Sprinkle both sides of steak with cracked black pepper, pressing into surface.

In a 12-inch skillet melt margarine or butter. Add steaks. Sprinkle with salt. Cook over medium-high heat to desired doneness, turning once. (Allow 12 to 14 minutes total cooking time for medium doneness.) Drain off fat. Transfer steaks to a serving platter; keep warm.

Pour brandy into skillet. Stir, scraping up browned bits. Bring to boiling.

Stir broth, cream, mustard, and peppercorns into skillet. Cook and stir over high heat for 2 or 3 minutes or till thickened. Pour over steaks. Makes 4 servings.

Nutrition facts per serving: 528 calories, 29 g total fat (12 g saturated fat), 172 mg cholesterol, 460 mg sodium, 3 g carbohydrate, 1 g fiber, 53 g protein.
Daily Value: 11% vitamin A, 6% vitamin C, 3% calcium, 44% iron.

PEPPER-BACON BURGERS

Heat rating: Hotter

The all-American burger just got spicy with the addition of serrano or jalapeño chili peppers.

1   beaten egg
¼   cup fine dry bread crumbs
6   slices crisp cooked bacon, crumbled
4   to 6 serrano or 2 to 3 jalapeño chili
      peppers, seeded and finely chopped
      (3 tablespoons)
2   tablespoons milk
1   pound lean ground beef
1   Anaheim or mild green chili pepper,
      seeded and cut into rings
1   small onion, thinly sliced and
      separated into rings
2   tablespoons margarine or butter
4   lettuce leaves
4   kaiser rolls or hamburger buns, split
      and toasted

In a large mixing bowl stir together egg, bread crumbs, bacon, serrano or jalapeño chili peppers, and milk. Add ground beef and mix well. Shape meat into four ¾-inch thick patties.

Grill patties, on an uncovered grill, directly over medium coals for 15 to 18 minutes or till no pink remains, turning once.

Meanwhile, in a small saucepan or skillet cook the chili pepper and onion in margarine or butter about 10 minutes or till onion is tender. Serve burgers on lettuce-lined buns. Top burgers with pepper-onion mixture. Makes 4 servings.

Nutrition facts per serving: 550 calories, 29 g total fat (9 g saturated fat), 132 g cholesterol, 733 mg sodium, 38 g carbohydrate, 1 g fiber, 32 g protein.
***Daily Value:** 11% vitamin A, 34% vitamin C, 8% calcium, 29% iron.*

ROAST TENDERLOIN WITH SPICY PAPAYA SAUCE

Heat rating: Hot

In the Caribbean, this dish would most likely be made with the hottest chili pepper of all—the habanero or Scotch Bonnet pepper. Serrano or jalapeño peppers work just as well and tone down the heat.

1   pound beef tenderloin
¼   teaspoon salt
¼   teaspoon ground red or ground
     black pepper
1   medium papaya, peeled, seeded, and
     finely chopped (1 cup)
¼   cup lime juice
2   small serrano chili peppers, seeded
     and chopped
⅛   teaspoon salt
⅛   teaspoon ground black pepper
¼   cup whipping cream

Trim fat from meat. Rub ¼ *teaspoon* salt and ¼ *teaspoon* red or black pepper onto meat. Place meat on a rack in a shallow roasting pan. Insert a meat thermometer. Roast, uncovered, in a 325° oven for 45 to 60 minutes for rare (140°) or 1 to 1¼ hours for medium (160°).

Meanwhile, for sauce, in a saucepan combine papaya, lime juice, chili peppers, ⅛ *teaspoon* salt, and ⅛ *teaspoon* black pepper. Stir in cream. Heat through over low heat.

To serve, slice meat into four portions. Serve sauce with meat. Makes 4 servings.

Nutrition facts per serving: 214 calories, 10 g total fat (5 g saturated fat), 101 mg cholesterol, 198 mg sodium, 5 g carbohydrate, 0 g fiber, 26 g protein.
Daily Value: 14% vitamin A, 44% vitamin C, 2% calcium, 9% iron.

PEPPERY POT ROAST

Heat rating: Hotter

Your family might dub this "pot roast with pizazz" thanks to the black pepper, red pepper, and hot pepper sauce. Any meat leftovers will make tasty sandwiches on hearty rye bread.

1   2½- to 3-pound boneless beef chuck
      pot roast
1   teaspoon ground black pepper
½   teaspoon ground red pepper
2   tablespoons cooking oil
¾   cup vegetable juice cocktail
½   to 1 teaspoon bottled hot
      pepper sauce
4   cloves garlic, halved
1   teaspoon instant beef bouillon
      granules
½   teaspoon dry mustard
2   medium sweet potatoes, peeled and
      quartered
8   small parsnips, halved crosswise
4   stalks celery, bias-sliced into
      1-inch pieces (2 cups)
1   medium onion, cut into wedges
½   cup cold water
¼   cup all-purpose flour
      Salt

Trim fat from meat. Rub black pepper and red pepper over surface of meat. In a 4- to 4½-quart Dutch oven brown meat on all sides in hot oil. Drain off fat.

In a medium mixing bowl stir together vegetable juice cocktail, hot pepper sauce, garlic, bouillon granules, and mustard. Pour over meat. Bring to boiling; reduce heat. Cover and simmer for 1 hour.

Add sweet potatoes, parsnips, celery, and onion to meat mixture. Cover and simmer for 45 to 60 minutes more or till meat is tender. Add water, if necessary, during cooking. Remove meat and vegetables from pan.

For gravy, skim fat from pan juices; measure juices and, if necessary, add enough water to equal 1½ cups. Combine the ½ cup cold water and flour. Stir into juices; return to pan. Cook and stir till thickened and bubbly. Cook and stir 1 minute more. Season to taste with salt. Slice meat. Serve gravy with meat and vegetables. Serves 8 to 10.

Nutrition facts per serving: 485 calories, 16 g total fat (6 g saturated fat), 143 mg cholesterol, 372 mg sodium, 33 g carbohydrate, 7 g fiber, 50 g protein.
Daily Value: 100% vitamin A, 52% vitamin C, 6% calcium, 44% iron.

PORK TENDERLOIN WITH RASPBERRY SAUCE

Heat rating: Hot

This special occasion dish shows off pork tenderloin with a spicy fruit sauce, fresh starfruit, and berries.
Choose a seedless jam for the prettiest appearance.

1   **pound pork tenderloin, cut into
      1-inch thick slices**
2   **tablespoons margarine or butter**
¼   **teaspoon ground black pepper**
⅓   **cup seedless raspberry or
      strawberry jam**
2   **tablespoons red wine vinegar**
2   **teaspoons prepared horseradish**
1   **clove garlic, minced**
¼   **teaspoon ground red pepper**
    Sliced star fruit (optional)
    Fresh raspberries (optional)

Pound the pork slices with the flat side of a meat mallet till ½ inch thick. In a 12-inch skillet melt margarine or butter over medium-high heat. Add pork slices to skillet and sprinkle with black pepper. Cook for 1 to 2 minutes per side or till light pink in center and juices run clear. Remove from skillet; keep warm.

For sauce, stir jam, vinegar, horseradish, garlic, and red pepper into skillet. Cook and stir till bubbly; cook about 1 minute more or till slightly thickened. Spoon sauce over pork slices. Garnish with star fruit and fresh raspberries, if desired. Makes 4 servings.

Nutrition facts per serving: 282 calories, 10 g total fat (3 g saturated fat), 81 mg cholesterol, 157 mg sodium, 22 g carbohydrate, 1 g fiber, 25 g protein.
Daily Value: 8% vitamin A, 14% vitamin C, 1% calcium, 12% iron.

GINGERED PORK RAGOUT WITH BABY CARROTS

Heat rating: Hotter

This one-pot meal really packs a punch! If you prefer to omit the wine, then increase the broth to 2 cups.

2	tablespoons cooking oil
1½	pounds boneless pork stew meat, cut into 1-inch cubes
1	tablespoon cooking oil
1	medium onion, chopped (½ cup)
1	medium leek, chopped
3	tablespoons finely chopped gingerroot
4	cloves garlic, minced
1	jalapeño chili pepper, finely chopped
2	tablespoons all-purpose flour
1	14½-ounce can diced tomatoes
1	cup chicken broth
1	cup dry white wine
1	teaspoon salt
½	teaspoon ground black pepper
8	ounces baby carrots
	Hot cooked noodles, couscous, or rice (optional)

In a Dutch oven heat *2 tablespoons* oil over medium-high heat. Add pork, *half* at a time, and cook about 5 minutes or till brown. Remove from Dutch oven; set aside.

Add *1 tablespoon* oil to Dutch oven. Add onion, leek, gingerroot, garlic, and chili pepper. Cook till onion is tender. Stir in flour. Add reserved pork, *undrained* tomatoes, broth, wine, salt, and black pepper. Bring to boiling.

Cover Dutch oven and place in a 350° oven. Bake about 45 minutes. Add carrots. Continue baking, uncovered, about 1 hour more or till meat is tender and mixture is thickened. If desired, serve with noodles, couscous, or rice. Makes 6 servings.

Nutrition facts per serving: 444 calories, 19 g total fat (5 g saturated fat), 74 mg cholesterol, 628 mg sodium, 35 g carbohydrate, 6 g fiber, 26 g protein. Daily Value: 92% vitamin A, 33% vitamin C, 6% calcium, 20% iron.

PORK SCALOPPINE WITH MUSTARD AND ROSEMARY

Heat rating: Hot

To keep the pork warm while you prepare the sauce, place the cooked pork slices on a warm serving platter. Cover with foil and place the platter in a 300° oven.

1 pound pork tenderloin
⅓ cup all-purpose flour
¼ teaspoon salt
½ teaspoon ground black pepper
2 tablespoons margarine or butter
1 tablespoon olive oil or cooking oil
1 cup sliced fresh mushrooms
2 cloves garlic, minced
1 tablespoon snipped fresh rosemary or
    1 teaspoon dried rosemary, crushed
¾ cup chicken broth
2 tablespoons Dijon-style mustard
1 teaspoon finely shredded lemon peel
1 tablespoon lemon juice
  Lemon wedges (optional)
  Fresh rosemary (optional)

Cut pork crosswise into ½-inch thick slices. Pound with the flat side of a meat mallet till about ⅛-inch thick. In a shallow dish combine flour, salt, and black pepper. Coat both sides of pork with seasoned flour, shaking off excess.

In a large skillet heat margarine or butter and oil over medium-high heat. Add *half* of the pork to skillet and cook about 2 minutes per side or till golden brown on the outside and light pink in center (juices will run clear). Remove from skillet and keep warm while cooking remaining pork. Set aside.

Reduce heat to medium. Add mushrooms, garlic, and rosemary. Cook and stir till mushrooms are just tender. Add broth, scraping up any browned bits. Bring to boiling. Boil for 5 minutes or till reduced by half. Stir in mustard, lemon peel, and lemon juice. Heat through. Spoon over pork. Garnish with lemon wedges and fresh rosemary, if desired. Makes 4 servings.

Nutrition facts per serving: 287 calories, 14 g total fat (3 g saturated fat), 81 mg cholesterol, 594 mg sodium, 10 g carbohydrate, 1 g fiber, 28 g protein.
Daily Value: 7% vitamin A, 7% vitamin C, 2% calcium, 16% iron.

Pork Chops with Szechwan Peppercorn Paste

Heat rating: Hot

Here's your chance to make a sensational spice blend of three kinds of pepper, coriander, garlic, citrus, and sesame oil. Make more than you need, store it in the refrigerator, and use it with other cuts of pork, chicken, or turkey.

1 teaspoon Szechwan peppercorns (optional)
1 tablespoon ground coriander
½ teaspoon crushed red pepper
3 cloves garlic, minced
2 teaspoons finely shredded lemon or lime peel
1 tablespoon lemon or lime juice
1 teaspoon toasted sesame oil
¼ teaspoon salt
¼ teaspoon coarsely ground black pepper
4 (about 2 pounds) pork loin rib chops, cut 1¼-inches thick
2 tablespoons finely snipped fresh cilantro or parsley
Lime wedges (optional)
Cilantro blossoms (optional)

Run peppercorns, if using, through a pepper mill or crush with a mortar and pestle. In a small baking pan stir together the peppercorns, coriander, and red pepper. Bake in a 350° oven for 10 minutes, stirring once. Remove from oven; cool for 10 minutes.

In a small mixing bowl stir together the roasted seasonings, garlic, lemon or lime peel, lemon or lime juice, sesame oil, salt, and black pepper.

Place pork chops in a single layer in a 13x9x2-inch baking pan. Spoon spice mixture evenly over chops and rub over both sides of each pork chop. Let stand at room temperature for 15 minutes.

Bake pork chops, uncovered, in a 375° oven for 25 to 30 minutes or till light pink in center and juices run clear. Sprinkle with cilantro or parsley. Garnish with lime wedges and cilantro blossoms, if desired. Makes 4 servings.

Nutrition facts per serving: 186 calories, 11 g total fat (3 g saturated fat), 61 mg cholesterol, 184 mg sodium, 3 g carbohydrate, 0 g fiber, 20 g protein.
Daily Value: 1% vitamin A, 7% vitamin C, 2% calcium, 8% iron.

GRILLED HAM STEAKS WITH SPICY APRICOT GLAZE

Heat rating: Hotter

Pineapple, plum, and apple jam or preserves make good substitutes for the apricot jam or preserves.

3   tablespoons apricot jam or preserves
2   tablespoons coarse-grain mustard
1   teaspoon cider vinegar
⅛   teaspoon ground red pepper
1   pound fully cooked boneless ham, cut into four ½-inch thick slices

For apricot glaze, in a small mixing bowl stir together apricot jam or preserves, mustard, vinegar, and red pepper.

Grill ham slices directly over hot coals for 8 to 10 minutes or till brown, turning once and brushing occasionally with apricot glaze. (Or, broil ham slices 5 inches from the heat for 8 to 10 minutes or till brown, turning once and brushing occasionally with apricot glaze.) Makes 4 servings.

Nutrition facts per serving: 190 calories, 6 g total fat (2 g saturated fat), 51 mg cholesterol, 1,273 mg sodium, 12 g carbohydrate, 0 g fiber, 21 g protein.
Daily Value: 0% vitamin A, 34% vitamin C, 1% calcium, 11% iron.

SOMBRERO RIBS WITH TORTILLAS
Heat rating: Hot

Serve these spicy Mexican-flavored pork ribs with rolled tortillas to help sop up every bit of the rich sauce. Before serving, wrap tortillas in foil and place in a 350° oven about 10 minutes or till heated. Roll up each warm tortilla and arrange on a serving plate.

8 ounces chorizo or hot pork sausage links, cut up
1 medium onion, sliced (¾ cup)
2 cloves garlic, minced
2½ pounds pork loin back ribs, cut into 2-rib sections
1 14½-ounce can diced or chopped tomatoes
1 cup beer or water
1 4-ounce can diced green chili peppers, drained
2 teaspoons instant beef bouillon granules
2 teaspoons dried oregano, crushed
½ teaspoon crushed red pepper
4 medium zucchini, cut into ½-inch thick slices (about 5¼ cups)
1 large green or red sweet pepper, cut into bite-size pieces (¾ cup)
⅓ cup cold water
3 tablespoons all-purpose flour
½ cup shredded cheddar cheese (2 ounces)
12 6-inch flour tortillas, warmed

In a Dutch oven cook sausage, onion, and garlic till sausage is brown. Drain. Remove sausage mixture from Dutch oven. In same pan brown ribs, half at a time, in sausage drippings.

Return sausage mixture and ribs to Dutch oven. Add *undrained* tomatoes, beer or water, chili peppers, bouillon granules, oregano, and red pepper. Bring to boiling; reduce heat. Cover and simmer for 50 minutes.

Add zucchini and sweet pepper to Dutch oven; cover and simmer 15 minutes more. With a slotted spoon, remove meats and vegetables to a platter; keep warm.

Skim off fat from pan juices. Measure juices. Add water, if necessary, to make 2 cups liquid; return to Dutch oven. Stir together cold water and flour. Stir into mixture in Dutch oven. Cook and stir till thickened and bubbly. Cook and stir 1 minute more.

Pour some of the sauce over meat and vegetable mixture on a serving platter. Sprinkle with cheese. Pass remaining sauce and warm tortillas. Makes 6 servings.

Nutrition facts per serving: 330 calories, 26 g total fat (10 g saturated fat), 37 mg cholesterol, 820 mg sodium, 33 g carbohydrate, 2 g fiber, 30 g protein.
Daily Value: 14% vitamin A, 50% vitamin C, 15% calcium, 19% iron.

ROAST PORK CALYPSO

Heat rating: Hot

This spicy grilled pork roast is served with a tropical fruit called a plantain. A plantain resembles a banana with a thick, green skin and a longer, more squared-off shape. Unlike bananas, you must cook plantains before eating them. Although their flavor is mild, these plantains are spiked with a chili pepper and brown sugar mixture.

3   cups hickory chips
1   5-pound pork center loin roast
¾   cup packed brown sugar
2   tablespoons dark rum or lime juice
2   cloves garlic, minced
2   fresh serrano or jalapeño chili peppers, seeded and finely chopped
1   teaspoon finely shredded lime peel
1   teaspoon ground ginger
¼   teaspoon salt
¼   teaspoon ground cloves
4   or 5 large ripe plantains
¼   cup margarine or butter
4   lime slices, halved
    Hot cooked wild rice (optional)

About 1 hour before cooking, soak hickory chips in enough water to cover; drain. Make a 1-inch deep slash between each rib on the meaty side of the roast, making about eight slashes in all.

In a small mixing bowl stir together brown sugar, rum or lime juice, garlic, chili peppers, lime peel, ginger, salt, and cloves. Stir till well combined. Set aside ¼ cup of spice mixture. Spoon about ½ teaspoon of the remaining spice mixture into each slash in the meat.

Insert a meat thermometer in center of roast, without touching bone or fat. Arrange medium coals around a drip pan. Test for medium-low heat above the pan. Add hickory chips to coals. Place roast on a grill rack over drip pan. Cover and grill about 2 hours or till meat thermometer registers 150°.

Meanwhile, tear off two 24x18-inch pieces of heavy-duty foil. Make a double thickness that measures 18x12-inches. Cut off ends of plantains. Peel and cut in half crosswise, then lengthwise. Place plantains in center of foil. Dot with margarine or butter. Spoon on some of the reserved spice mixture. Seal foil, leaving room for steam to build. Place foil packets on grill over coals when meat thermometer registers 150°. Spread remaining spice mixture over top of roast.

Grill meat and plantains for 15 minutes more or till thermometer registers 160°. To serve, insert lime slices into slashes in roast. Serve with wild rice, if desired. Makes 10 servings.

Nutrition facts per serving: 304 calories, 11 g total fat (3 g saturated fat), 44 mg cholesterol, 148 mg sodium, 36 g carbohydrate, 2 g fiber, 15 g protein.
Daily Value: 13% vitamin A, 30% vitamin C, 1% calcium, 8% iron.

CURRIED PORK STEW

Heat rating: Hotter

Look for chili oil (also called hot oil or hot pepper oil) in the Oriental section of your supermarket, at an Oriental market, or a specialty food store. If you use cooking oil instead of chili oil, then increase the ground red pepper to ¼ teaspoon.

1 tablespoon chili oil or cooking oil
12 ounces lean boneless pork, cut into ¾-inch cubes
1 medium onion, chopped (½ cup)
2 cloves garlic, minced
1 tablespoon curry powder
1 teaspoon grated gingerroot
⅛ teaspoon ground red pepper
¼ cup water
1 tablespoon all-purpose flour
1 14½-ounce can diced or chopped tomatoes
2 medium carrots, sliced (1 cup)
1 medium sweet potato, peeled and cut into bite-size pieces
¼ cup mixed dried fruit bits
¼ cup snipped fresh parsley
¼ cup chopped peanuts

In a large skillet heat oil over medium-high heat. Cook meat, onion, and garlic in oil till meat is brown and onion is tender. Stir in curry powder, gingerroot, and red pepper. Cook and stir 1 minute more.

In a 2-quart round casserole stir together water and flour. Add *undrained* tomatoes, carrots, sweet potato, and dried fruit bits. Add meat mixture; stir till well combined.

Cover and bake in a 350° oven about 1 hour or till meat is tender. If desired, season to taste with salt. To serve, sprinkle each serving with parsley and peanuts. Makes 4 servings.

Nutrition facts per serving: 324 calories, 16 g total fat (4 g saturated fat), 44 g cholesterol, 450 mg sodium, 30 g carbohydrate, 4 g fiber, 18 g protein.
Daily Value: 184% vitamin A, 56% vitamin C, 7% calcium, 16% iron.

BAKED HAM WITH MUSTARD GLAZE

Heat rating: Hot

This sweet and tangy sauce can be made with other mustards, such as hot mustard or spicy brown mustard.

1	4-pound fully cooked boneless ham
½	cup apple or pineapple juice
⅓	cup prepared mustard
¼	cup packed brown sugar
¼	cup molasses
1½	teaspoons dry mustard
¼	teaspoon ground red pepper
¼	cup fine dry bread crumbs
1	tablespoon margarine or butter, melted

Place ham on a rack in a shallow baking pan. Score top of ham in a diamond pattern, making cuts about ¼-inch deep. Insert a meat thermometer. Bake in a 325° oven for 1½ to 2 hours or till thermometer registers 120°.

Meanwhile, in a small mixing bowl stir together juice, prepared mustard, brown sugar, molasses, dry mustard, and red pepper. For sauce, place *half* of the mixture in a small saucepan.

Spoon *half* of the remaining mustard mixture over top of ham. Bake 15 minutes more; spoon the remaining mustard mixture over ham. Combine bread crumbs and melted margarine. Sprinkle over top of ham. Return to oven. Bake about 15 minutes more or till thermometer registers 140°. Meanwhile, bring sauce to boiling. Remove from heat and pass sauce with ham. Makes 16 servings.

Nutrition facts per serving: 209 calories, 7 g total fat (2 g saturated fat), 60 mg cholesterol, 1,450 mg sodium, 10 g carbohydrate, 0 g fiber, 24 g protein.
Daily Value: 0% vitamin A, 39% vitamin C, 2% calcium, 14% iron.

PEPPERY GLAZED PORK CHOPS

Heat rating: Hotter

Instead of pork chops, try this with a 1⅓- to 1¾-pound boneless pork loin roast and cut into 1 inch thick slices before cooking.

4 boneless pork loin chops, cut 1 to
     1¼ inches thick
2 tablespoons soy sauce
2 tablespoons molasses
1 tablespoon cracked black pepper
1 tablespoon brown sugar
1 teaspoon ground coriander
¼ teaspoon crushed red pepper
2 cloves garlic, minced

Place pork chops in a shallow dish. For marinade, in a small mixing bowl stir together soy sauce, molasses, cracked pepper, brown sugar, coriander, red pepper, and garlic. Pour over pork chops. Marinate at room temperature for 20 to 30 minutes.

Drain pork chops, reserving marinade. Line a shallow baking pan with foil. Place chops on a rack in pan and bake, uncovered, in a 375° oven for 30 to 40 minutes or till light pink in center and juices run clear.

For glaze, transfer marinade to a small saucepan; bring to boiling. Boil gently about 1 minute or till slightly thickened. Transfer chops to a serving plate. Spoon glaze over chops. Makes 4 servings.

Nutrition facts per serving: 48 calories, 0 g total fat (0 g saturated fat), 0 mg cholesterol, 519 mg sodium, 12 g carbohydrate, 0 g fiber, 1 g protein.
Daily Value: 0% vitamin A, 2% vitamin C, 2% calcium, 7% iron.

ITALIAN LAMB STEW

Heat rating: Hot

Fresh fennel, used in this stew, is a popular ingredient in Italian cooking. Fennel has a light, licoricelike flavor and celerylike texture. When cooked, the flavor becomes more delicate and the texture softens. Look for fennel in your grocer's produce section.

1½ pounds lean boneless lamb, cut into
   ¾-inch pieces
1 tablespoon cooking oil
4 shallots, chopped
3 cloves garlic, minced
3 medium carrots, cut into 1-inch
   pieces
3 cups beef broth
1 10-ounce can chopped tomatoes and
   green chili peppers
½ cup dry red wine
2 tablespoons grated fresh horseradish
   or prepared horseradish
½ teaspoon salt
¼ teaspoon ground black pepper
2 medium zucchini or yellow summer
   squash, sliced
1 medium fennel bulb, sliced
¼ cup cold water
3 tablespoons cornstarch
1 tablespoon snipped fresh basil
1 tablespoon snipped fresh oregano

In a Dutch oven brown the lamb, half at a time, in hot oil. Add more oil, if necessary. Remove meat from pan and set aside.

Cook shallots and garlic till tender. Return all meat to pan; add carrots, broth, tomatoes, wine, horseradish, salt, and black pepper. Bring to boiling; reduce heat. Cover and simmer for 45 minutes.

Stir in fennel and zucchini or summer squash. Return to boiling; reduce heat. Cover and simmer about 15 minutes more or till meat and vegetables are tender.

In a small mixing bowl stir together cold water and cornstarch; add to pan. Cook and stir till thickened and bubbly. Cook and stir 2 minutes more. Stir in fresh basil and oregano just before serving. Makes 6 servings.

Nutrition facts per serving: 293 calories, 16 g total fat (6 g saturated fat), 63 mg cholesterol, 849 mg sodium, 14 g carbohydrate, 2 g fiber, 19 g protein.
Daily Value: 96% vitamin A, 19% vitamin C, 5% calcium, 15% iron.

LAMB CURRY

Heat rating: Hot

The hotness of this dish depends on the type of curry powder you use. Imported curry powder from specialty food shops tends to be hotter than grocery store curry powder.

1   pound boneless lamb, cut into
     ¾-inch cubes
1   tablespoon cooking oil
1   large onion, chopped (1 cup)
4   cloves garlic, minced
2   tablespoons curry powder
2   medium apples, peeled, cored,
     and thinly sliced
1   cup chicken broth
¼   cup shredded coconut
¼   cup raisins
2   tablespoons brown sugar
2   tablespoons Worcestershire sauce
¼   teaspoon finely shredded lime peel
¼   cup cold water
2   tablespoons all-purpose flour
2   cups hot cooked rice
     Condiments such as chopped peanuts,
        sliced bananas, pineapple chunks,
        sliced green onions, and chutney
        (optional)

In a large saucepan brown *half* of the meat in hot oil. Remove from pan. Brown remaining meat with onion and garlic. Stir in curry powder. Cook and stir for 1 minute. Return all meat to pan.

Stir in apples, broth, coconut, raisins, brown sugar, Worcestershire sauce, and lime peel. Bring to boiling; reduce heat. Cover and simmer about 45 minutes or till meat is tender. Stir cold water into flour; stir into saucepan. Cook and stir till thickened and bubbly. Cook and stir 1 minute more. Serve over rice. If desired, pass condiments. Makes 4 servings.

Nutrition facts per serving: 488 calories, 20 g total fat (8 g saturated fat), 64 mg cholesterol, 320 mg sodium, 57 g carbohydrate, 4 g fiber, 22 g protein.
Daily Value: 0% vitamin A, 33% vitamin C, 5% calcium, 30% iron.

STIR-FRIED CHICKEN WITH THAI CHILI PEPPER PASTE

Heat rating: Hotter

Kaffir lime leaves give this dish a fresh, enticing flavor. Look for the leaves at Southeast Asian markets.

1   tablespoons cooking oil
2   cloves garlic, minced
¼   cup Homemade Thai Chili
       Pepper Paste (see recipe below)
1   pound boneless, skinless chicken
       thighs, cut into bite-size pieces
1   cup vegetable broth
1   cup chicken broth
8   ounces fresh long beans or green
       beans, trimmed and cut into bite-
       size pieces, or one 9- or 10-ounce
       package frozen cut green beans,
       thawed and drained
2   tablespoons fish sauce
2   fresh kaffir lime leaves or 1 teaspoon
       finely shredded lime peel
      Hot cooked Thai sticky rice or short
       grain rice
      Lemon slices (optional)
      Lime peel strips (optional)

Preheat a wok or large skillet over medium-high heat. Add oil. Add garlic and stir-fry for 1 minute. Add Homemade Thai Chili Pepper Paste and stir-fry for 1 minute, pressing paste against the sides and bottom of wok or skillet. Add chicken and stir-fry for 2 minutes or till light brown.

Add vegetable broth and chicken broth to wok or skillet. Bring to boiling. Add long or green beans, fish sauce, and kaffir lime leaves or lime peel. Return to boiling; reduce heat. Simmer, uncovered, for 5 minutes.

If using kaffir lime leaves, discard them. Serve chicken mixture with sticky or short grain rice. Garnish with lemon slices and lime peel strips, if desired. Makes 4 servings.

Homemade Thai Chili Pepper Paste: In a large mortar or small mixing bowl place 1 large *shallot,* finely chopped; 2 cloves *garlic,* minced; 1 tablespoon grated *gingerroot;* 1-inch piece *lemon grass,* finely chopped or ¼ teaspoon finely shredded *lemon peel;* 4 to 6 small *dried hot red chili peppers* (such as de arbol or cayenne), finely chopped, or 2 teaspoon *crushed red pepper;* 1 snipped fresh *kaffir lime leaf* or ½ teaspoon finely shredded *lime peel;* 1 teaspoon *shrimp paste;* ¼ teaspoon *salt;* and ⅛ teaspoon *ground black pepper.* Using a pestle or the back of a spoon, crush mixture till it forms a paste. Makes about ⅓ cup.

Nutrition facts per serving: 200 calories, 8 g total fat (2 g saturated fat), 65 mg cholesterol, 1,131 mg sodium, 10 g carbohydrate, 2 g fiber, 25 g protein.
Daily Value: 15% vitamin A, 13% vitamin C, 4% calcium, 13% iron.

INDIAN OVEN-FRIED CHICKEN STRIPS

Heat rating: Hot

Serve these spicy chicken strips with a cool and creamy dipping sauce. Simply combine 1½ cups plain yogurt and 2 tablespoons chopped fresh mint.

1½ **pounds boneless, skinless chicken breast halves**
3 **tablespoons margarine or butter**
1 **teaspoon curry powder**
½ **to ¾ teaspoon ground red pepper**
½ **cup dry roasted peanuts**
⅓ **cup coconut**
¼ **cup yellow cornmeal**
1 **teaspoon paprika**
¼ **teaspoon salt**
¼ **teaspoon ground black pepper**

Rinse chicken and pat dry. Cut chicken lengthwise into ½-inch-wide strips; place in a medium mixing bowl.

In a small saucepan melt butter or margarine over medium heat. Stir in curry powder and red pepper. Pour over chicken and toss to coat.

In a blender container or food processor bowl combine peanuts and coconut. Cover and blend or process till peanuts are ground. Transfer to a pie plate or shallow bowl. Stir in cornmeal, paprika, salt, and black pepper.

Coat chicken strips with peanut mixture. Place in a single layer on ungreased baking sheets.

Bake, uncovered, in a 375° oven for 10 to 15 minutes or till chicken is no longer pink. Makes 6 servings.

Nutrition facts per serving: 274 calories, 16 g total fat (16 g saturated fat), 59 mg cholesterol, 281 mg sodium, 0 g carbohydrate, 1 g fiber, 23 g protein.
Daily Value:10% vitamin A, 1% vitamin C, 1% calcium, 9% iron.

CHICKEN PAELLA WITH PEPPERS

Heat rating: Hot

Our tasters held different opinions as to whether this dish was hot enough with 1 dried chili pepper.
For those who can stand the heat, increase the peppers according to your tolerance.

1½ pounds meaty chicken pieces (breasts, thighs, drumsticks)
2 tablespoons cooking oil
6 ounces chorizo links or hot Italian sausage links, sliced ½ inch thick
1 large onion, cut into wedges
1 medium red sweet pepper, cut into 1-inch squares (¾ cup)
1 dried pasilla or cascabel chili pepper, seeded and chopped
3 cloves garlic, minced
⅛ teaspoon thread saffron
2 cups hot chicken or vegetable broth
¾ cup long grain rice
½ teaspoon ground turmeric
½ teaspoon ground cumin
1 10-ounce package frozen peas, thawed
½ cup Calamata or ripe olives, pitted and halved

Rinse chicken and pat dry. Season with salt and black pepper. In a 12-inch skillet or 4-quart Dutch oven cook chicken in hot oil, uncovered, over medium heat for 10 to 15 minutes or till brown, turning chicken to brown evenly. Remove chicken, reserve drippings.

Cook sausage, onion, sweet pepper, chili pepper, and garlic in reserved drippings over medium-low heat about 10 minutes or till sausage is done. Drain off fat.

Crush saffron. Add saffron, broth, rice, turmeric, and cumin to skillet. Bring to boiling, scraping up browned bits. Place chicken on top. Reduce heat. Cover and simmer about 20 minutes or till chicken is no longer pink. Turn chicken once during cooking.

Add peas and olives to chicken mixture. Cover and cook about 5 minutes more or till heated through and rice is tender. Serves 4.

Nutrition facts per serving: 499 calories, 37 g total fat (10 g saturated fat), 78 mg cholesterol, 597 mg sodium, 45 g carbohydrate, 4 g fiber, 45 g protein.
Daily Value: 24% vitamin A, 67% vitamin C, 6% calcium, 29% iron.

RED CHILI CHICKEN WITH GOAT CHEESE

Heat rating: Hotter

Depending on who will be eating this fire-breathing dish, it may be more appropriate to serve it as an appetizer so each person gets a smaller portion (8 appetizer servings instead of 4 main-dish servings).

3   dried chipotle chili peppers
2   dried pasilla chili peppers
1   cup chicken broth
1   medium onion, coarsely
      chopped (½ cup)
1   medium red sweet pepper, roasted*
1   jalapeño chili pepper, seeded
      and chopped
2   cups chopped cooked chicken
      or turkey
5   ounces goat cheese
1   tablespoon cooking oil
1   medium yellow and/or green sweet
      pepper, cut into strips
1   medium onion, halved and sliced
8   6-inch corn or flour tortillas, warmed

Remove stems and seeds from chipotle and pasilla peppers; coarsely chop. In a saucepan combine dried peppers and broth. Bring to boiling. Remove from heat. Cover and let stand for 30 minutes.

Pour broth mixture in a blender container or food processor bowl. Add onion, roasted sweet pepper, and jalapeño pepper. Cover and blend or process till slightly chunky. Return mixture to saucepan. Simmer, uncovered, for 10 minutes.

Spread about ½ cup of the pepper mixture in the bottom of a 2-quart square baking dish. Spoon chicken over pepper mixture. Pour remaining pepper mixture over chicken. Crumble goat cheese over chicken and pepper mixture. Bake, uncovered, in a 350° oven about 20 minutes or till mixture is heated through and bubbly.

Meanwhile, in a small saucepan heat oil over medium heat, add sweet pepper strips and sliced onion; cook for 2 to 3 minutes or until onion is tender. Serve with warm tortillas and top with sweet peppers and onion. Makes 4 servings.

*To roast peppers, halve the pepper. Remove stems, membranes, and seeds. Place sweet peppers, cut side down, on a foil-lined baking sheet. Bake in a 425° oven for 20 to 25 minutes or till skin is bubbly and browned. Place the peppers in a new brown paper bag; seal and let stand for 20 to 30 minutes or till cool enough to handle. Pull the skin off gently and slowly using a paring knife.

Nutrition facts per serving: 451 calories, 21 g total fat (8 g saturated fat), 99 mg cholesterol, 633 mg sodium, 33 g carbohydrate, 2 g fiber, 34 g protein.
Daily Value: 27% vitamin A, 96% vitamin C, 13% calcium, 16% iron.

BROILED TURKEY WITH CASHEW-MULATO CHILI SAUCE

Heat rating: Hot

Cashew butter gives this sauce a nutty richness. Look for it at a health food store or use ½ cup peanut butter as an easy substitute.

3 dried mulato or ancho chili peppers
1 cup chicken broth
½ cup cashew butter or peanut butter
2 cloves garlic, quartered
1 tablespoon brown sugar
1 tablespoon coarsely chopped gingerroot
1 tablespoon soy sauce
½ cup half-and-half or light cream
3 or 4 turkey breast tenderloin steaks (about 1 pound total)
Green onion brush (optional)

Slit chili peppers open and remove stems and seeds. Place in a single layer on a baking sheet. Roast in a 450° oven for 1 minute. Meanwhile, in a medium saucepan bring broth to a boil. Add roasted chili peppers. Remove from heat. Cover and let stand for 30 minutes.

For sauce, place chili peppers and broth in a food processor or blender container. Cover and process or blend till smooth. Add cashew butter or peanut butter, garlic, brown sugar, gingerroot, and soy sauce. Cover and blend till well combined. With machine running, slowly add half-and-half or cream. Process till smooth. Transfer mixture to saucepan. Heat over low heat while cooking turkey.

Rinse turkey and pat dry. Place turkey on the unheated rack of a broiler pan. Season with salt and black pepper. Broil turkey, 4 or 5 inches from the heat for 5 minutes. Turn and broil for 3 to 5 minutes more or till tender and no longer pink.

To serve, spoon sauce over plates. Diagonally slice turkey tenderloins. Arrange turkey slices over sauce. Garnish with green onion brushes, if desired. Makes 4 servings.

Nutrition facts per serving: 193 calories, 7 g total fat (3 g saturated fat), 61 mg cholesterol, 604 mg sodium, 7 g carbohydrate, 1 g fiber, 24 g protein.
Daily Value: 13% vitamin A, 1% vitamin C, 4% calcium, 10% iron.

ROAST TURKEY WITH BLUE CORNMEAL CHORIZO STUFFING

Heat rating: Hotter

Spoon any stuffing that doesn't fit in the bird into a casserole. Cover and chill. Bake, covered, during the last 30 minutes with the turkey.

1 pound bulk chorizo sausage or
   bulk Italian sausage
1 cup chopped celery
1 medium onion, chopped (½ cup)
½ cup chopped carrot
4 to 6 serrano or jalapeño chili peppers,
   seeded and finely chopped
4 cloves garlic, minced
½ teaspoon dried thyme, crushed
½ teaspoon dried sage, crushed
6 cups coarsely crumbled Blue Corn
   Bread
½ cup chicken broth
1 8- to 10-pound turkey
   Cooking oil or melted margarine
   or butter

For stuffing, in a large skillet cook sausage, celery, onion, carrot, chili peppers, and garlic over medium heat about 10 minutes or till sausage is brown and vegetables are tender. Drain off fat. Stir in thyme and sage.

In a large mixing bowl stir together crumbled corn bread and sausage mixture. Add broth, tossing till well combined.

Rinse turkey well and pat dry. Rub salt inside the body cavity. To stuff, spoon some of the stuffing loosely into the neck cavity; fasten the neck skin to the back with a small skewer. Lightly spoon some of the stuffing into body cavity. Tie drumsticks securely to the tail and twist the wing tips under the back.

Place the stuffed bird, breast side up, on a rack in a shallow roasting pan. Brush the bird with cooking oil. Roast, uncovered, in a 325° oven for 3½ to 4½ hours or till tender and no longer pink and thermometer inserted in inner thigh (not touching bone) registers 180°. Makes 8 to 10 servings.

Blue Corn Bread: In a small skillet cook ¼ cup *margarine or butter* and 2 cloves *garlic,* minced till garlic is tender. In a medium mixing bowl stir together 1½ cups *blue or yellow cornmeal,* ½ cup *all-purpose flour,* 2 tablespoons *sugar,* 1 tablespoon *baking powder,* and ½ teaspoon *salt.* In another medium mixing bowl stir together 2 *eggs,* 1 cup *milk,* and margarine-garlic mixture. Add to cornmeal mixture. Stir just till batter is smooth. Pour into a greased 9x9x2-inch baking pan. Bake in a 425° oven for 20 to 25 minutes or till a toothpick inserted near the center comes out clean. Cool in pan on a wire rack.

Nutrition facts per serving: 626 calories, 43 g total fat (14 g saturated fat), 210 mg cholesterol, 588 mg sodium, 50 g carbohydrate, 3 g fiber, 82 g protein.
Daily Value: 42% vitamin A, 24% vitamin C, 20% calcium, 39% iron.

TORTILLA-CRUSTED CHICKEN WITH SOUR CREAM

Heat rating: Hot

Serve this crunchy Southwest-inspired chicken dish with tall glasses of mint-flavored iced tea or frosty margaritas.

1½ cups finely crushed tortilla chips
      (about 6 ounces)
¼ cup all-purpose flour
1 teaspoon ground cumin
¼ teaspoon salt
¼ to ½ teaspoon ground red pepper
2 eggs, beaten
2 tablespoons milk
1 2½- to 3-pound broiler-fryer chicken,
      cut up
   Dairy sour cream

In a shallow dish stir together crushed tortilla chips, flour, cumin, salt, and red pepper. In a small mixing bowl stir together eggs and milk.

Skin chicken. Rinse chicken and pat dry. Dip chicken pieces in egg mixture and coat in tortilla mixture. Place chicken, meaty side up, in a single layer in a 15x10x1-inch or 13x9x2-inch baking pan so pieces don't touch.

Bake chicken, uncovered, in a 375° oven for 45 to 55 minutes or till tender and no longer pink. *Do not* turn. Serve with sour cream. Makes 6 servings.

Nutrition facts per serving: 393 calories, 21 g total fat (7 g saturated fat), 143 mg cholesterol, 361 mg sodium, 24 g carbohydrate, 2 g fiber, 26 g protein.
Daily Value: 10% vitamin A, 0% vitamin C, 6% calcium, 15% iron.

SOUTHEAST ASIAN CHICKEN SOUP

Heat rating: Hot

Chili peppers, rice sticks, and hard-cooked egg give this chicken-noodle soup its Asian flare.

12 ounces boneless, skinless chicken
    breast halves
2 cloves garlic, minced
1 tablespoon grated gingerroot
3 hot chili peppers, such as serrano
    or jalapeño, seeded and
    finely chopped
1 tablespoon cooking oil
½ teaspoon ground coriander
½ teaspoon ground cumin
¼ teaspoon ground turmeric
4 cups chicken broth
2 ounces rice sticks, broken
2 teaspoons lemon juice
¼ cup thinly sliced green onions
1 hard-cooked egg, coarsely chopped

Rinse chicken and pat dry. Cut into bite-size pieces. In a large saucepan cook garlic, gingerroot, and chili peppers in oil over medium-high heat for 15 seconds.

Stir in coriander, cumin, and turmeric. Add chicken. Cook and stir for 2 to 3 minutes or till chicken is browned. Carefully add chicken broth and rice sticks; bring to boiling. Reduce heat. Cover and simmer for 5 minutes. Stir in lemon juice. Sprinkle with green onion and hard-cooked egg. Makes 4 servings.

Nutrition facts per serving: 243 calories, 9 g total fat (2 g saturated fat), 99 mg cholesterol, 1111 mg sodium, 15 g carbohydrate, 0 g fiber, 25 g protein.
Daily Value: 4% vitamin A, 55% vitamin C, 3% calcium, 16% iron.

SPICY CHICKEN SATÉ WITH PEANUT SAUCE

Heat rating: Hotter

Serve this spicy saté and peanut sauce with a cool, crisp cucumber relish. Combine 2 thinly sliced cucumbers, ¼ cup sliced green onion, and 1 clove minced garlic. Toss with a combination of ½ cup rice wine vinegar, 2 tablespoons sugar, and ¼ teaspoon salt. Chill 2 to 24 hours.

1 pound boneless, skinless chicken breast halves
2 tablespoons cooking oil
3 cloves garlic, minced
1 teaspoon finely shredded lime peel
2 tablespoons lime juice
1 tablespoon curry powder
1 teaspoon granulated sugar or honey
1 teaspoon soy sauce
¾ teaspoon ground red pepper
1 medium onion, chopped (½ cup)
2 cloves garlic, minced
1 tablespoon cooking oil
1 cup cream of coconut
½ cup milk
½ cup peanut butter
2 tablespoons lime juice
2 tablespoons brown sugar
1 tablespoon soy sauce
¾ teaspoon ground red pepper
½ teaspoon curry powder
2 inches stick cinnamon
2 cups hot cooked rice

Soak 8 bamboo skewers in hot water for 1 to 3 hours. (Or, use metal skewers and omit soaking.) Rinse chicken and pat dry. Cut lengthwise into strips.

For marinade, in a plastic bag combine *2 tablespoons* oil, *3 cloves* garlic, lime peel, *2 tablespoons* lime juice, *1 tablespoon* curry powder, granulated sugar or honey, *1 teaspoon* soy sauce, and *¾ teaspoon* red pepper. Add chicken. Seal bag and marinate in the refrigerator for 2 hours.

Meanwhile, for peanut sauce, in a medium saucepan cook onion and *2 cloves* garlic in *1 tablespoon* oil till onion is tender. Stir in cream of coconut, milk, peanut butter, *2 tablespoons* lime juice, brown sugar, *1 tablespoon* soy sauce, *¾ teaspoon* red pepper, and *½ teaspoon* curry powder. Add stick cinnamon. Cook and stir over low heat for 10 to 15 minutes or till desired consistency. Remove from heat and discard stick cinnamon.

Drain chicken; discard marinade. Loosely thread chicken strips accordion-style onto skewers. Grill directly over medium-hot coals for 5 to 7 minutes or till chicken is tender and no longer pink. Serve with peanut sauce and rice. Makes 4 servings.

Nutrition facts per serving: 1093 calories, 80 g total fat (17 g saturated fat), 62 mg cholesterol, 593 mg sodium, 63 g carbohydrate, 3 g fiber, 34 g protein.
Daily Value: 6% vitamin A, 14% vitamin C, 8% calcium, 26% iron.

NORTH INDIAN CHICKEN WITH YOGURT

Heat rating: Hot

What makes this dish North Indian? The unique blend of flavors from gingerroot, allspice, cinnamon, red pepper, curry powder, and lemon juice.

4 chicken drumsticks
4 chicken thighs
1 teaspoon grated gingerroot
½ teaspoon ground allspice
½ teaspoon ground cinnamon
½ teaspoon crushed red pepper
¼ teaspoon curry powder
2 cloves garlic, minced
1 tablespoon lemon juice

Rinse chicken and pat dry. In a small mixing bowl stir together gingerroot, allspice, cinnamon, red pepper, curry powder, and garlic. Stir in lemon juice till a paste forms.

Loosen skin of chicken, but do not remove. Rub paste mixture under skin of chicken. Rub any remaining paste over skin of chicken.

Grill chicken pieces, with bone side up, directly over medium coals for 20 minutes. Turn and grill for 15 to 25 minutes more or till tender and no longer pink. Makes 4 servings.

Nutrition facts per serving: 235 calories, 12 g total fat (3 g saturated fat), 99 mg cholesterol, 97 mg sodium, 2 g carbohydrate, 0 g fiber, 28 g protein.
***Daily Value:** 5% vitamin A, 4% vitamin C, 1% calcium, 10% iron.*

WEST AFRICAN CHICKEN STEW

Heat rating: Hot

Peanut butter thickens and flavors this hearty chicken stew served over rice. All you need is a fresh green salad to complete your meal.

1   2½- to 3-pound broiler-fryer chicken, cut up
4   shallots, chopped
4   cloves garlic, minced
2   tablespoons cooking oil
2   hot chili peppers (such as serrano or jalapeño), seeded and chopped
1   14½-ounce can chopped tomatoes
4   carrots, sliced ½-inch thick (2 cups)
2   cups chicken broth
1   tablespoon lime juice
2   inches stick cinnamon
¼   teaspoon ground nutmeg
⅛   teaspoon ground cloves
1   red sweet pepper, chopped (¾ cup)
½   cup peanut butter
1   tablespoon cornstarch
2   cups chopped fresh spinach leaves
2   cups hot cooked rice

Rinse chicken and pat dry. In a 4-quart Dutch oven cook chicken, shallots, garlic, and chili peppers in hot oil about 15 minutes or till chicken is brown, turning chicken to brown evenly. Drain off fat.

Add *undrained* tomatoes, *1½ cups* of the carrots, chicken broth, lime juice, stick cinnamon, nutmeg, and cloves. Bring to boiling; reduce heat. Cover and simmer for 20 minutes. Add chopped sweet pepper. Cover and simmer for 10 to 15 minutes more or till chicken is tender and no longer pink.

In a small mixing bowl stir together the remaining *½ cup* chicken broth, peanut butter, and cornstarch. Add to chicken mixture. Cook and stir till thickened and bubbly. Cook and stir 2 minutes more.

Stir in spinach. Cover and simmer 5 minutes or till wilted. To serve, spoon rice into soup bowls. Ladle stew over rice. Makes 4 servings.

Nutrition facts per serving: 693 calories, 36 g total fat (8 g saturated fat), 99 mg cholesterol, 871 mg sodium, 48 g carbohydrate, 6 g fiber, 46 g protein.
Daily Value: 227% vitamin A, 116% vitamin C, 10% calcium, 5% iron.

CHILI POWDER NUGGETS WITH CILANTRO CREAM

Heat rating: Hot

Sliced summer tomatoes and cucumbers make a refreshing accompaniment to these gunpowder nuggets. Try them as a tasty appetizer too, but double the cilantro cream sauce for dipping.

¼ cup cornflake crumbs or fine dry bread crumbs
1 tablespoon chili powder
½ teaspoon ground black pepper
¼ teaspoon salt
¼ teaspoon ground red pepper
1 pound boneless, skinless chicken breast halves
2 tablespoons margarine or butter, melted
½ cup dairy sour cream
2 tablespoons snipped fresh cilantro

In a plastic bag combine crumbs, chili powder, black pepper, salt, and red pepper.

Rinse chicken and pat dry. Cut chicken into 1-inch pieces. In a medium mixing bowl toss chicken pieces with melted margarine or butter. Place in bag with crumb mixture. Seal bag and shake till chicken is well coated.

Place chicken pieces in a single layer on a lightly greased baking sheet. Bake in a 400° oven for 8 to 10 minutes or till tender and no longer pink, turning pieces once.

Meanwhile, for cilantro cream, in a small mixing bowl stir together sour cream and cilantro. Serve with chicken. Makes 4 servings.

Nutrition facts per serving: 252 calories, 15 g total fat (6 g saturated fat), 72 mg cholesterol, 324 mg sodium, 5 g carbohydrate, 1 g fiber, 23 g protein.
Daily Value: *25% vitamin A, 5% vitamin C, 4% calcium, 8% iron.*

FOUR-PEPPER CHILI WITH TURKEY

Heat rating: Hotter
Poblano, jalapeño, serrano, and chipotle chili peppers all team up to fire up this blazing pot of chili.

2	pounds ground raw turkey
1	large onion, chopped (1 cup)
6	cloves garlic, minced
2	tablespoons cumin seed
1	large green sweet pepper, chopped (1 cup)
1	large red sweet pepper, chopped (1 cup)
2	poblano chili peppers, seeded and chopped
2	jalapeño chili peppers, seeded and chopped
2	serrano chili peppers, seeded and chopped
3	14½-ounce cans chopped tomatoes
2	cups chicken broth
1	cup dark beer
1	7-ounce can chipotle chili peppers in adobo sauce, coarsely chopped
2	tablespoons chili powder
1	tablespoon ground coriander
1	tablespoon coarsely cracked black pepper
1	teaspoon ground cinnamon
1	ounce coarsely chopped unsweetened chocolate
	Dairy sour cream
	Snipped fresh cilantro

In a 5-quart Dutch oven cook turkey, onion, garlic, and cumin till onion is tender and turkey is no longer pink. Drain off fat. Stir in sweet peppers, poblano peppers, jalapeño peppers, and serrano peppers. Cook and stir for 5 minutes.

Add *undrained* tomatoes, chicken broth, beer, chipotle peppers, chili powder, coriander, cracked black pepper, and cinnamon. Bring to boiling; reduce heat. Simmer, uncovered, for 30 to 45 minutes.

Just before serving, stir in chocolate. Dollop each serving with sour cream and sprinkle with cilantro. Makes 8 to 10 servings.

Nutrition facts per serving: 296 calories, 16 g total fat (5 g saturated fat), 49 mg cholesterol, 821 mg sodium, 19 g carbohydrate, 3 g fiber, 20 g protein.
Daily Value: 31% vitamin A, 162% vitamin C, 10% calcium, 31% iron.

ROAST CHICKEN BREASTS WITH MUSTARD

Heat rating: Hotter

Slip a spicy mustard mixture under the skin of chicken breasts, pop them in the oven, and sit back and wait for a great chicken dish.

2   tablespoons spicy brown mustard
2   tablespoons honey mustard
3   thinly sliced green onions
2   tablespoons snipped parsley
¼   teaspoon ground red pepper
3   cloves garlic, minced
6   medium chicken breast halves
    (2¼ pounds)
    Cooking oil

In a small mixing bowl stir together spicy brown mustard, honey mustard, green onion, parsley, red pepper, and garlic.

Rinse chicken and pat dry. Loosen skin on breasts. Spread mustard mixture evenly under the skin of the chicken breasts. Secure skin to breast with toothpicks or small skewers.

Place breasts in a 3-quart rectangular baking dish. Lightly brush with cooking oil. Sprinkle with salt and ground black pepper. Bake, uncovered, in a 375° oven for 45 to 55 minutes or till tender and no longer pink. Makes 6 servings.

Nutrition facts per serving: 273 calories, 12 g total fat (3 g saturated fat), 66 mg cholesterol, 475 mg sodium, 17 g carbohydrate, 1 g fiber, 23 g protein.
Daily Value: 4% vitamin A, 11% vitamin C, 3% calcium, 10% iron.

CHICKEN MOLE

Heat rating: Hotter

Mole is a spicy Mexican dish that means a sauce made with chili peppers. This well-seasoned version is made with a combination of dried ancho or mulato chili peppers and fresh jalapeño peppers.

4	dried ancho or mulato chili peppers
1	teaspoon cumin seed
1	teaspoon anise seed
1	teaspoon sesame seed
½	teaspoon whole cloves
1	2½- to 3-pound broiler-fryer chicken, cut up
2	tablespoons cooking oil
½	cup chicken broth
1	8-ounce can tomatoes
1	medium onion, coarsely chopped (½ cup)
¼	cup slivered almonds
3	jalapeño chili peppers, seeded and chopped
2	cloves garlic
¼	teaspoon ground cinnamon
⅛	teaspoon ground nutmeg
½	ounce coarsely chopped semisweet chocolate
2	cups hot cooked rice
¼	cup pumpkin or sesame seeds, toasted (optional)

Remove seeds and stems from chili peppers. Coarsely chop peppers. Set aside.

In a small dry skillet toast cumin seed, anise seed, sesame seed, and cloves over low heat about 3 minutes or till very aromatic and very lightly browned. Place in a blender container. Cover and blend till ground. Set aside.

Rinse chicken and pat dry. Season with salt and ground black pepper. In a 12-inch skillet or Dutch oven cook chicken pieces in hot oil over medium heat for 10 to 15 minutes or till light brown, turning to brown evenly. Remove from skillet or Dutch oven; drain off fat.

For mole sauce, to ground spice mixture in blender container add chili peppers, chicken broth, *undrained* tomatoes, onion, almonds, jalapeño peppers, garlic, cinnamon, and nutmeg. Cover and blend to a coarse purée. Transfer mixture to skillet or Dutch oven. Add chocolate. Cook and stir over low heat till chocolate melts.

Add chicken to mole sauce. Cover and simmer for 25 to 30 minutes or till chicken is tender and no longer pink, turning pieces once.

To serve, transfer chicken to a serving platter with rice. Skim fat from sauce. Pour mole sauce over chicken and rice. Garnish with toasted pumpkin or sesame seeds, if desired. Makes 6 servings.

Nutrition facts per serving: 353 calories, 18 g total fat (4 g saturated fat), 66 mg cholesterol, 247 mg sodium, 22 g carbohydrate, 2 g fiber, 24 g protein.
Daily Value: 14% vitamin A, 30% vitamin C, 4% calcium, 19% iron.

FORTY-CLOVE GARLIC CHICKEN

Heat rating: Hot

Relax! The garlic cloves mellow during cooking and contribute only a hint of garlic to the food (and your breath).

3 pounds meaty chicken pieces
    (thighs, breasts, and drumsticks)
2 tablespoons cooking oil
40 cloves garlic, unpeeled
½ cup dry white wine
2 tablespoons lemon juice
2 teaspoons cracked black pepper
⅛ to ¼ teaspoon ground red pepper
    Chicken broth
    French bread (optional)
    Hot cooked pasta (optional)

Skin chicken, if desired. Rinse chicken and pat dry. Sprinkle lightly with salt. In a 12-inch skillet heat oil over medium heat. Add chicken pieces, placing meaty pieces toward the center of the skillet. Cook, uncovered, about 15 minutes, turning to brown evenly. Drain off fat.

Add *unpeeled* garlic cloves, wine, lemon juice, and cracked black pepper to skillet. Sprinkle chicken with red pepper. Bring to boiling; reduce heat. Cover and simmer for 35 to 40 minutes or till chicken is tender and no longer pink.

Remove chicken and garlic to a serving platter; keep warm. Measure juices from skillet. Add enough chicken broth to skillet juices to equal 1 cup.

For sauce, in the skillet melt margarine or butter over medium-low heat. Stir in flour. Add reserved juices. Cook and stir till thickened and bubbly. Cook and stir 1 minute more. Spoon sauce over chicken. Serve with pasta, if desired.

To eat garlic, squeeze the unpeeled clove between your thumb and index finger till the clove pops out of its peel. You can eat the garlic clove whole or spread it over slices of French bread, if desired. Makes 6 servings.

Nutrition facts per serving: 350 calories, 18 g total fat (4 g saturated fat), 104 mg cholesterol, 270 mg sodium, 8 g carbohydrate, 1 g fiber, 36 g protein.
Daily Value: 4% vitamin A, 15% vitamin C, 4% calcium, 13% iron.

ORIENTAL CHICKEN SOUP

Heat rating: Hotter
Lemon peel and an ancho chili pepper give a sophisticated zing to this easy-to-fix cream soup.

12 ounces boneless, skinless chicken
    breast halves
1 14½-ounce can chicken broth
½ cup water
1 tablespoon fish sauce
1½ teaspoons finely shredded lemon peel
½ teaspoon ground red pepper
¼ teaspoon ground coriander
1 cup whipping cream
1 dried ancho chili pepper, coarsely
    chopped
2 tablespoons coconut, toasted

Rinse chicken and pat dry. Cut into bite-size pieces. In a large saucepan stir together chicken broth, water, fish sauce, lemon peel, red pepper, and coriander. Bring to boiling. Add chicken. Reduce heat. Cover and simmer for 5 to 10 minutes or till chicken is no longer pink.

Stir in whipping cream. Heat through. Sprinkle each serving with chili peppers and toasted coconut. Makes 4 servings.

Nutrition facts per serving: 333 calories, 26 g total fat (15 g saturated fat), 128 mg cholesterol, 540 mg sodium, 4 g carbohydrate, 0 g fiber, 20 g protein.
Daily Value: 30% vitamin A, 2% vitamin C, 4% calcium, 6% iron.

HOISIN HENS

Heat rating: Hot

Hoisin sauce is a thick and flavorful Oriental ingredient made from soybeans, sugar, garlic, flour, vinegar, and spices. Look for it at your grocery store with other Oriental ingredients or at an Oriental market.

2   1- to 1½-pound Cornish game hens
½   cup hoisin sauce
¼   cup raspberry or red wine vinegar
¼   cup orange juice
1   to 2 teaspoons chili paste

Rinse hens and pat dry. Using a sharp knife or kitchen shears, halve hens lengthwise. Season cavities with salt. Place hens, breast side up, on a rack in a shallow roasting pan. Cover loosely with foil. Roast in a 375° oven about 30 minutes.

Meanwhile, in a small mixing bowl stir together hoisin sauce, vinegar, orange juice, and chili paste. Brush some of the mixture over hens. Roast, uncovered, for 45 to 60 minutes more or till hens are tender and no longer pink, brushing with remaining hoisin sauce mixture occasionally. Makes 4 servings.

Nutrition facts per serving: 371 calories, 23 g total fat (5 g saturated fat), 120 mg cholesterol, 2223 mg sodium, 6 g carbohydrate, 0 g fiber, 38 g protein.
Daily Value: *0% vitamin A, 13% vitamin C, 0% calcium, 5% iron.*

FIVE-SPICE TURKEY BREAST

Heat rating: Hot

If you don't have any chili oil on hand, use cooking oil and add ¼ teaspoon ground red pepper to the dry spice mixture.

1 2½- to 3½-pound turkey breast half
   with bone
2 tablespoons chili oil
½ teaspoon ground cinnamon
½ teaspoon ground allspice
½ teaspoon curry powder
¼ teaspoon ground nutmeg
¼ teaspoon ground ginger
   Steamed pea pods (optional)

Rinse turkey and pat dry. Insert small skewers or wooden toothpicks to hold the skin and meat together along the bottom edge of the breast half. Brush oil over turkey breast. In a small mixing bowl stir together cinnamon, allspice, curry powder, nutmeg, and ginger. Rub spice mixture over turkey.

Place turkey, skin side up, on a rack in a shallow roasting pan. Insert a meat thermometer into center of breast. Cover the turkey loosely with foil.

Roast turkey in a 325° oven for 1½ to 2 hours or till meat thermometer registers 170°. Remove foil the last 30 minutes of roasting. Spoon drippings over turkey occasionally.

Cover the turkey with foil; let stand 15 minutes before carving. Slice to serve. Serve slices on a bed of steamed pea pods, if desired. Makes 6 servings.

Nutrition facts per serving: 221 calories, 12 g total fat (3 g saturated fat), 70 mg cholesterol, 59 mg sodium, 0 g carbohydrate, 0 g fiber, 27 g protein.
Daily Value: 0% vitamin A, 0% vitamin C, 2% calcium, 9% iron.

SPICY CHICKEN AND NOODLES

Heat rating: Hot

The addition of hot chili peppers updates this all-American classic.

- 1 5- to 6-pound stewing chicken or two 2½- to 3-pound broiler-fryer chickens, cut up
- 4 stalks celery with leaves, cut up (2⅔ cups)
- 1 large onion, cut up (1 cup)
- 1 large carrot, cut up (¾ cup)
- 12 whole black peppercorns
- 4 sprigs cilantro
- 1½ teaspoons salt
- 1 teaspoon dried marjoram, crushed
- ½ to 1 teaspoon ground white pepper
- 6 cups water
- 1 8-ounce package frozen egg noodles
- 2 serrano or jalapeño chili peppers, seeded and chopped
- 2 cloves garlic, minced
- 2 cups thinly sliced zucchini, yellow summer squash, or carrot
- 1 cup sliced chopped celery
- ½ cup cold water
- ¼ cup all-purpose flour
   Fresh oregano (optional)

In a large kettle or 4- or 5-quart Dutch oven combine chicken, celery stalks, onion, cut-up carrot, peppercorns, cilantro, salt, marjoram, and white pepper. Add water. Bring to boiling; reduce heat. Cover and simmer stewing chicken for 2 to 2½ hours or till chicken is tender. (Simmer broiler-fryers for 1 hour or till tender.)

Remove from heat. Remove chicken. Line a sieve with several layers of 100% cotton cheesecloth. Set sieve over a large mixing bowl. Ladle broth through sieve. Discard cheesecloth and vegetables. Use a metal spoon to skim fat that rises to the surface of the broth. Measure broth. (You should have about 6 cups; add water if necessary to make 6 cups.)

When chicken is cool enough to handle, remove meat from bones and chop. Discard skin and bones.

In the kettle, bring broth to boiling. Add noodles, chili peppers, and garlic. Cover and reduce heat. Simmer about 15 minutes. Add zucchini, summer squash, or sliced carrot, and sliced celery; return to boiling; reduce heat and simmer about 15 minutes more or till noodles and vegetables are tender. Add chicken. Combine ½ cup cold water and flour. Add to broth mixture, mixing well. Cook and stir till thickened and bubbly. Cook and stir 1 minute more. Garnish with fresh oregano, if desired. Makes 8 servings.

Nutrition facts per serving: 425 calories, 22 g total fat (6 g saturated fat), 106 mg cholesterol, 525 mg sodium, 21 g carbohydrate, 2 g fiber, 34 g protein.
Daily Value: 20% vitamin A, 17% vitamin C, 4% calcium, 20% iron.

SPICY SALMON EN CROÛTE WITH LEMON-CHIVE SAUCE

Heat rating: Hot

For a special dinner, try this mildly-spiced salmon and spinach enclosed in a flaky crust.

1   10-ounce package frozen chopped
    spinach
2   shallots, chopped
4   serrano or jalapeño chili peppers,
    seeded and chopped
2   cloves garlic, minced
1   tablespoon margarine or butter
¼   cup fine dry bread crumbs
1   beaten egg yolk
¼   teaspoon dried dillweed
¼   teaspoon ground black pepper
⅛   teaspoon salt
2   cups water
2¾ pounds skinless salmon fillets
    (¾- to 1-inch thick)
½   of a 17½-ounce package (1 sheet)
    frozen puff pastry, thawed
1   beaten egg
1   tablespoon water
    Lemon-Chive Sauce (see recipe below)
    Lemon wedges (optional)
    Fresh dill (optional)

For filling, cook spinach according to package directions. Drain well, pressing out excess liquid; set aside. In a skillet cook the shallots, chili peppers, and garlic in margarine or butter till tender. Stir in bread crumbs, egg yolk, dillweed, black pepper, and salt. Stir in spinach.

In a large skillet bring water to boiling. Carefully add fish. Return to boiling, then reduce heat. Cover and simmer gently for 2 minutes (fish will not be done). Carefully, remove fish from water. Pat fish dry with paper towels. Lay fillets side by side. On a lightly floured surface roll pastry into a rectangle about 4 inches longer than the length of the fillets and twice the width plus 4 inches.

To assemble, transfer pastry to an ungreased 15x10x1-inch baking pan. On *half* of the rectangle, spread *half* of the filling to within 1 inch of edges. Top with fish, then remaining filling. In a mixing bowl combine egg and water; brush some onto pastry edges. Bring pastry over fish. Seal edges with the tines of a fork. Brush top with remaining egg mixture. Bake, uncovered, in a 400° oven for 20 to 25 minutes or till golden brown. Serve warm with Lemon-Chive Sauce. Garnish with lemon wedges and fresh dill, if desired. Makes 6 servings.

Lemon-Chive Sauce: In a small saucepan melt 2 tablespoons *margarine or butter*. Stir in 2 tablespoons *all-purpose flour*. Add 1 cup *milk* all at once. Cook and stir till thickened and bubbly. Cook and stir 1 minute more. Remove from heat. Stir in 1 tablespoon finely snipped *fresh chives* and 1 teaspoon finely shredded *lemon peel*. Serve warm. Makes about 1 cup.

Nutrition facts per serving: 502 calories, 28 g total fat (4 g saturated fat), 111 mg cholesterol, 480 mg sodium, 25 g carbohydrate, 0 g fiber, 36 g protein.
Daily Value: 50% vitamin A, 34% vitamin C, 11% calcium, 16% iron.

TNT TILAPIA

Heat rating: Hotter

Tilapia (tuh-LAHP-ee-uh) is a lean freshwater fish with a mild and subtly sweet flavor. Try it with this spicy cornmeal coating.

2   tablespoons all-purpose flour
2   tablespoons cornmeal
1   tablespoon chili powder
2   teaspoons ground cumin
1½ to 2 teaspoons ground red pepper
1   teaspoon salt
½   teaspoon paprika
¼   teaspoon ground black pepper
1   pound tilapia fillets (½ to ¾ inches thick), cut into four serving-size portions
3   tablespoons cooking oil
    Fresh cilantro (optional)

In a shallow dish stir together flour, cornmeal, chili powder, cumin, red pepper, salt, paprika, and black pepper. Rinse fish and pat dry. Dip fish into flour mixture.

In a 12-inch skillet heat the oil over medium heat. Add fish to the skillet, trying not to overlap. Fry for 4 to 8 minutes or till fish flakes easily when tested with a fork and coating is golden brown, turning once. (Allow 4 to 6 minutes per ½-inch thickness.) Remove fish from skillet and drain on paper towels. Garnish with fresh cilantro, if desired. Makes 4 servings.

Nutrition facts per serving: 219 calories, 12 g total fat (2 g saturated fat), 43 mg cholesterol, 618 mg sodium, 9 g carbohydrate, 1 g fiber, 19 g protein.
Daily Value: 12% vitamin A, 5% vitamin C, 3% calcium, 16% iron.

SEAFOOD GUMBO

Heat rating: Hotter

The Cajuns invented gumbo when they tried to duplicate a French fish stew called bouillabaisse. This spicy gumbo is brimming with crab, shrimp, fish, and vegetables.

1 pound fresh or frozen skinless red snapper or catfish fillets (½ to 1 inch thick)

12 ounces fresh or frozen cooked split crab legs

8 ounces fresh or frozen shelled shrimp

½ cup margarine or butter

½ cup all-purpose flour

2 medium onions, chopped (1 cup)

1 cup chopped green sweet pepper

1 cup chopped red sweet pepper

5 cloves garlic, minced

4 serrano or jalapeño chili peppers, seeded and chopped

4 cups chicken broth

2 14½-ounce cans chopped tomatoes

1 teaspoon dried thyme, crushed

½ teaspoon ground red pepper

¼ teaspoon ground black pepper

1 bay leaf

2 cups sliced fresh okra or one 10-ounce package frozen cut okra, thawed

4 cups hot cooked rice

Thaw fish, crab, and shrimp, if frozen. Cut fish fillets into 1-inch pieces. Remove crabmeat from shells, then cut crabmeat into bite-size pieces. Devein shrimp. Cover and refrigerate fish shellfish till needed.

For gumbo, in a 5-quart heavy Dutch oven melt margarine or butter. Stir in flour. Cook and stir over medium heat for 20 to 25 minutes or till dark reddish brown.

Add onions, sweet peppers, garlic, and chili peppers. Continue cooking and stirring over medium heat for 5 to 10 minutes or till vegetables are very tender.

Gradually stir in chicken broth. Stir in *undrained* tomatoes, thyme, red pepper, black pepper, and bay leaf. Bring to boiling; reduce heat. Cover and simmer for 30 minutes.

Add okra, fish, crab, and shrimp. Return just to boiling; reduce heat. Cover and simmer for 2 to 5 minutes or till shrimp turns pink and fish flakes easily when tested with a fork. Remove and discard bay leaf. To serve, spoon rice into individual soup bowls. Ladle gumbo over rice. Makes 8 servings.

Nutrition facts per serving: 402 calories, 14 g total fat (3 g saturated fat), 85 mg cholesterol, 764 mg sodium, 41 g carbohydrate, 2 g fiber, 28 g protein.
Daily Value: 34% vitamin A, 107% vitamin C, 10% calcium, 24% iron.

PEPPERY CATFISH WITH PROSCIUTTO AND LEEKS

Heat rating: Hot

Leeks resemble oversized green onions and have a subtle onion flavor. You can substitute easier-to-find onions (2 medium) for the leeks, if desired.

4   8- to 10-ounce fresh or frozen pan-
      dressed catfish
2   medium leeks, sliced
1   beaten egg
¼   cup buttermilk
⅓   cup yellow cornmeal
2   tablespoons all-purpose flour
2   teaspoons coarsely cracked
      black pepper
½   teaspoon crushed red pepper
¼   teaspoon salt
¼   teaspoon ground white pepper
2   ounces thinly sliced prosciutto,
      chopped or 3 slices bacon, crisp-
      cooked and crumbled
1   tablespoon cooking oil
¼   cup cooking oil
      Lemon (optional)

Thaw fish, if frozen. Rinse and pat dry with paper towels. Halve leeks lengthwise and wash well. Cut into ¼-inch thick slices. Set aside.

In a shallow dish stir together egg and buttermilk. In another shallow dish stir together cornmeal, flour, cracked black pepper, red pepper, salt, and white pepper. Dip fish into egg mixture. Coat fish in cornmeal mixture. Set aside.

In a 12-inch skillet cook prosciutto or bacon and leeks in *1 tablespoon* hot oil over medium heat for 5 to 7 minutes or till leeks are tender. Remove from skillet.

In same skillet heat *¼ cup* cooking oil over medium heat. Add 2 pieces of the fish. Fry for 5 to 7 minutes or till golden. Turn carefully. Fry for 5 to 7 minutes more or till golden and crisp and fish flakes easily when tested with a fork.

Drain on paper towels. Arrange fish and leek mixture in a shallow baking pan. Place pan in a 300° oven to keep warm while frying remaining fish. Repeat frying with remaining fish, adding more oil, if necessary.

To serve, arrange fish on a platter. Spoon leek mixture over fish. Serve with lemon, if desired. Makes 4 servings.

Nutrition facts per serving: 516 calories, 34 g total fat (6 g saturated fat), 145 mg cholesterol, 540 mg sodium, 18 g carbohydrate, 3 g fiber, 34 g protein.
Daily Value: 7% vitamin A, 8% vitamin C, 5% calcium, 20% iron.

POACHED SNAPPER WITH HORSERADISH-GARLIC SAUCE

Heat rating: Hot

This rich-tasting horseradish and garlic sauce is ideal with fish steaks such as salmon or halibut. Or, try it with juicy grilled beef steaks.

4   1-inch thick salmon or halibut steaks
    (about 1¼ pounds)
1   cup vegetable or chicken broth
3   cloves garlic, minced
1   tablespoon margarine or butter
2   teaspoons all-purpose flour
⅛   teaspoon salt
¼   cup half and half or light cream
1   beaten egg yolk
1   tablespoon snipped fresh parsley
1   tablespoon prepared horseradish
1   teaspoon lemon juice
¼   teaspoon ground white pepper
    Parsley sprigs (optional)

Thaw fish, if frozen. Rinse fish and pat dry with paper towels.

In a 10-inch skillet bring vegetable or chicken broth to boiling; add fish. Add more broth, if necessary, to half-cover fish. Return to boiling; reduce heat. Cover and simmer for 8 to 12 minutes or till fish flakes easily when tested with a fork. Transfer fish to a warm serving platter, reserving broth. Keep fish warm. Strain broth, reserving ½ cup for sauce.

For sauce, in a small saucepan cook garlic in margarine or butter till tender. Stir in flour and salt. Add reserved broth and half-and-half or light cream. Cook and stir till thickened and bubbly. Cook and stir 1 minute more. Gradually stir half of the hot mixture into egg yolk. Return all to saucepan. Cook and stir till mixture is just bubbly. Reduce heat; cook and stir for 1 to 2 minutes more.

Remove sauce from heat. Stir in parsley, horseradish, lemon juice, and white pepper. Serve sauce over fish. Garnish with parsley, if desired. Makes 4 servings.

Nutrition facts per serving: 200 calories, 11 g total fat (3 g saturated fat), 84 mg cholesterol, 351 mg sodium, 3 g carbohydrate, 0 g fiber, 22 g protein.
Daily Value: 17% vitamin A, 5% vitamin C, 3% calcium, 8% iron.

MUSTARD FISH IN PHYLLO

Heat rating: Hot

When preparing this elegant fish entrée, be prepared to assemble the fish in phyllo as soon as you remove the partially cooked fish rolls from the oven.

4 fresh or frozen flounder, sole, pike,
    or walleye fillets (about 1 pound)
3 ounces sliced cold smoked red salmon
1 3-ounce package cream cheese,
    softened
¼ cup Dijon-style mustard
1 teaspoon mustard seed
8 sheets frozen phyllo dough
    (18x14-inch rectangles), thawed
½ cup margarine or butter, melted

Thaw fish, if frozen. Rinse and pat dry with paper towels. Place *one-fourth* of the sliced smoked salmon on top of *each* fish fillet. Sprinkle with black pepper. Roll up jelly-roll style.

Place rolls, seam side down, in an 8x8x2-inch baking dish. Cover and bake in a 350° oven about 20 minutes. (Fish will not be done.)

Meanwhile, in a mixing bowl combine cream cheese, mustard, and mustard seed. Remove fish rolls from baking dish; pat dry with paper towels.

Using four phyllo sheets and *3 tablespoons* margarine or butter, stack phyllo, brushing each sheet generously with margarine or butter. Halve phyllo stacks lengthwise.

Spread about *2 tablespoons* of the mustard mixture over one fish roll. Place fish roll near one end of phyllo strip. Carefully lift short end of phyllo over roll, pressing it against fish. Roll up, folding in the sides as you roll. Brush end of phyllo strip with a little margarine or butter; press to seal. Place roll, seam side down, on a rack in a 2-quart baking dish. Repeat with second fish roll.

Spread and wrap remaining fish rolls, using remaining phyllo sheets, *3 tablespoons* of the margarine or butter, and remaining mustard mixture.Make 3 diagonal slits in the top layers of each roll. Brush with remaining margarine or butter. Bake, uncovered, in a 400° oven for 20 to 25 minutes or till golden. Makes 4 servings.

Nutrition facts per serving: 532 calories, 36 g total fat (10 g saturated fat), 82 mg cholesterol, 1142 mg sodium, 22 g carbohydrate, 0 g fiber, 29 g protein.
Daily Value: 38% vitamin A, 0% vitamin C, 4% calcium, 13% iron.

SHRIMP WITH SERRANOS

Heat rating: Hotter

In a pinch use dried herbs in place of the fresh. Add them at the same time you add the shrimp, using ¼ teaspoon dried basil, crushed and ¼ teaspoon dried oregano, crushed.

1	pound fresh or frozen shrimp, peeled and deveined
3	tablespoons olive oil or cooking oil
¼	cup chopped red sweet pepper
3	serrano chili peppers, seeded and chopped
3	cloves garlic, minced
2	shallots, chopped
¼	cup shredded fresh Parmesan cheese
1	teaspoon snipped fresh basil
1	teaspoon snipped fresh oregano
	Hot cooked spaghetti (optional)

Thaw shrimp, if frozen. Rinse shrimp and pat dry with paper towels. In a 10-inch skillet heat oil over medium-high heat. Add shrimp, sweet pepper, chili peppers, garlic, and shallots. Cook and stir about 3 minutes or till shrimp turn pink.

Add Parmesan cheese, basil, and oregano; toss till well combined. Serve over spaghetti, if desired. Makes 4 servings.

Nutrition facts per serving: 194 calories, 13 g total fat (2 g saturated fat), 136 mg cholesterol, 231 mg sodium, 3 g carbohydrate, 0 g fiber, 17 g protein.
Daily Value: 17% vitamin A, 50% vitamin C, 7% calcium, 15% iron.

CHILI CRAB CAKES WITH CHIPOTLE MAYONNAISE

Heat rating: Hot

Chipotle chili peppers, which are dried and smoked jalapeño peppers, come conveniently canned in liquid. Look for them in the Mexican food aisle of your grocery store.

½ cup mayonnaise or salad dressing
1 canned chipotle chili pepper, drained and finely chopped
½ cup fresh or frozen corn kernels
¼ cup finely chopped green onion
1 teaspoon ground coriander
¼ teaspoon crushed red pepper
2 tablespoons margarine or butter
3 beaten eggs
⅔ cup fine dry bread crumbs
2 6-ounce cans crabmeat, drained, flaked, and cartilage removed
3 tablespoons fine dry bread crumbs
3 tablespoons cornmeal
3 tablespoons cooking oil
Lemon wedges (optional)

For chipotle mayonnaise, in a small mixing bowl stir together mayonnaise or salad dressing and chipotle chili pepper. Cover and refrigerate till needed.

For crab cakes, in a medium saucepan cook corn, green onion, coriander, and red pepper in margarine or butter till corn is tender, about 5 minutes.

In a medium mixing bowl stir together eggs, *⅔ cup* bread crumbs, and crabmeat. Stir in corn mixture. Using about *⅓ cup* crab mixture for *each,* shape into eight ½-inch thick patties. In a shallow dish stir together *3 tablespoons* bread crumbs and cornmeal. Coat patties with cornmeal mixture.

In a large skillet heat cooking oil over medium heat. Add *half* of the patties. Cook for 2 to 3 minutes per side or till golden brown. Drain on paper towels. Keep warm in a 300° oven while frying the remaining patties. Serve warm with chipotle mayonnaise and, if desired, lemon wedges. Makes 4 servings.

Nutrition facts per serving: 614 calories, 46 g total fat (8 g saturated fat), 245 mg cholesterol, 750 mg sodium, 27 g carbohydrate, 2 g fiber, 26 g protein.
Daily Value: 17% vitamin A, 12% vitamin C, 11% calcium, 17% iron.

CRAWFISH ÉTOUFFÉE

Heat rating: Hotter

Although this classic Cajun dish is most often made with crawfish, shrimp makes an equally delicious option.

1 pound fresh or frozen peeled crawfish
    tails or medium shrimp
2 large onions, finely chopped
1 cup finely chopped celery
½ cup finely chopped green
    sweet pepper
2 cloves garlic, minced
¼ cup cooking oil, margarine, or butter
2 tablespoons margarine or butter
4 teaspoons cornstarch
1 cup water
½ cup tomato sauce
½ teaspoon salt
½ teaspoon ground red pepper
¼ teaspoon ground black pepper
2 cups hot cooked rice

Thaw crawfish tails or shrimp, if frozen. In a heavy 3-quart saucepan cook onions, celery, sweet pepper, and garlic, covered, in the *¼ cup* oil, margarine, or butter about 10 minutes or till tender.

Add *2 tablespoons* margarine or butter, stirring till melted. Stir in cornstarch. Add crawfish or shrimp, water, tomato sauce, salt, red pepper, and black pepper.

Bring to boiling; reduce heat. Simmer, uncovered about 5 minutes or till crawfish are tender or shrimp turn pink. Serve with rice. Serves 4.

Nutrition facts per serving: 313 calories, 21 g total fat (3 g saturated fat), 174 mg cholesterol, 769 mg sodium, 12 g carbohydrate, 2 g fiber, 20 g protein.
Daily Value: 18% vitamin A, 31% vitamin C, 6% calcium, 22% iron.

GRILLED BLACKENED SWORDFISH

Heat rating: Hotter

Two important things are needed as you cook this peppery fish: 1. A cast iron skillet 2. Good ventilation.

2   **8- to 10-ounce fresh or frozen swordfish steaks, cut ¾ to 1 inch thick**
¾   **teaspoon ground white pepper**
¾   **teaspoon ground black pepper**
½   **teaspoon ground red pepper**
½   **teaspoon dried thyme, crushed**
½   **teaspoon onion powder**
½   **teaspoon garlic powder**
¼   **teaspoon salt**
3   **tablespoons margarine or butter, melted**
     Fresh thyme (optional)

Thaw fish, if frozen. Halve each steak to get 4 serving-size portions. Rinse fish and pat dry with paper towels.

In a shallow bowl stir together white pepper, black pepper, red pepper, thyme, onion powder, garlic powder, and salt.

Brush fish with some of the melted margarine or butter. Coat each fish portion evenly on both sides with pepper mixture.

Remove grill rack. Place a cast-iron 12-inch skillet directly on hot coals. Heat 5 minutes or till a drop of water sizzles when added to skillet.

Add fish to hot skillet. Drizzle with remaining margarine or butter. Cook, uncovered, for 3 to 4 minutes on each side or till fish flakes easily when tested with a fork. If desired, garnish with fresh thyme. Makes 4 servings.

To cook indoors: Prepare as above, *except* cook in a well-ventilated area. Turn on exhaust fan. Cook fish in a hot skillet on the range top over high heat for 3 to 4 minutes per side or till fish flakes easily when tested with a fork. Avoid breathing fumes.

Nutrition facts per serving: 219 calories, 13 g total fat (3 g saturated fat), 45 mg cholesterol, 336 mg sodium, 1 g carbohydrate, 0 g fiber, 23 g protein.
Daily Value: 15% vitamin A, 2% vitamin C, 1% calcium, 8% iron.

LINGUINE WITH HABANERO WHITE CLAM SAUCE

Heat rating: Hottest

If the thought of eating habanero chili peppers, the hottest in the world, puts you in a sweat, then try less intense New Mexico or serrano peppers in this sauce.

1   8-ounce package linguine
2   6½-ounce cans minced clams
    Light cream, half-and-half, or milk
½   cup sliced green onion
3   cloves garlic, minced
1   habanero chili pepper, seeded and
    finely chopped
2   tablespoons margarine or butter
¼   cup all-purpose flour
½   teaspoon dried oregano, crushed
¼   teaspoon salt
¼   teaspoon ground black pepper
¼   cup snipped fresh parsley
¼   cup dry white wine
¼   cup grated Parmesan cheese
    Parsley Sprigs (optional)

Cook linguine according to package directions. Drain well. Set aside.

Meanwhile, drain clams, reserving liquid from one can. Add enough light cream, half-and-half, or milk to reserved liquid to make 2 cups.

For sauce, in medium saucepan cook green onion, garlic, and chili pepper in margarine or butter till onions are tender.

Stir flour, oregano, salt, and black pepper into onion mixture. Add cream mixture all at once. Cook and stir till thickened and bubbly. Cook and stir 1 minute more.

Stir in clams, *¼ cup* parsley, and wine. Heat through. Serve clam sauce over hot linguine and sprinkle with Parmesan cheese. Garnish with parsley sprigs, if desired. Makes 4 servings.

Nutrition facts per serving: 560 calories, 21 g total fat (10 g saturated fat), 78 mg cholesterol, 466 mg sodium, 60 g carbohydrate, 1 g fiber, 28 g protein.
Daily Value: 37% vitamin A, 49% vitamin C, 22% calcium, 141% iron.

RED LENTIL TOSTADAS

Heat rating: Hotter

Lentils come in three colors: red, green, and brown. Look for the red ones at a health food or specialty food shop. Feel free to substitute green or brown lentils, if desired.

1   cup red lentils
2   cups vegetable or chicken broth
1   medium onion, chopped (½ cup)
3   jalapeño or serrano chili peppers, seeded and chopped
2   cloves garlic, minced
1   tablespoon cooking oil
1   teaspoon ground cumin
½   cup hot taco sauce or picante sauce
     Cooking oil
6   6-inch corn tortillas
1½   cups shredded lettuce
1   cup shredded cheddar or Monterey Jack cheese (4 ounces)
1   medium tomato, chopped (⅔ cup)
⅓   cup sliced pitted ripe olives

Rinse lentils; drain. In a 2-quart saucepan combine broth and lentils. Bring to boiling; reduce heat. Cover and simmer for 15 to 20 minutes or till lentils are tender and liquid is absorbed.

Meanwhile, in a medium skillet cook onion, chili peppers, and garlic in hot oil till onion is tender. Add cumin; cook and stir 1 minute more. Add onion mixture and taco or picante sauce to cooked lentils. Keep warm.

In a heavy skillet heat about ¼-inch of cooking oil. Fry tortillas, one at a time, in hot oil about 30 seconds on each side or till crisp and golden brown. Drain on paper towels. Keep tortillas warm in 300° oven while frying remaining tortillas.

To assemble tostadas, place tortillas on 6 individual plates. Dividing ingredients equally among tortillas, layer ingredients in the following order: lentil mixture, lettuce, cheese, tomato, and olives. Makes 6 servings.

Nutrition facts per serving: 323 calories, 16 g total fat (5 g saturated fat), 20 mg cholesterol, 598 mg sodium, 36 g carbohydrate, 3 g fiber, 13 g protein.
Daily Value: 11% vitamin A, 36% vitamin C, 19% calcium, 26% iron.

PESTO POTATO WEDGES WITH CANNELLINI-TOMATO SAUCE

Heat rating: Hotter

This hot and spicy meatless meal can really heat up your mouth even though the starchy potatoes help neutralize some of the heat.

1½ pounds potatoes
1 tablespoon margarine or butter
¼ teaspoon salt
¼ teaspoon ground black pepper
¼ cup milk
1 small zucchini, chopped (1 cup)
1 small yellow summer squash, chopped (1 cup)
¼ cup chopped shallots or onion
2 cloves garlic, minced
1 habanero or Scotch bonnet or 3 serrano chili peppers, seeded and chopped
1 tablespoon olive oil or cooking oil
2 cups meatless spaghetti sauce
1 15-ounce can white cannellini beans, rinsed and drained
1 egg
3 tablespoons purchased pesto
   Fresh basil (optional)

Peel and quarter potatoes. Cook, covered, in a small amount of boiling water for 20 to 25 minutes or till tender. Drain. Mash with a potato masher or beat with an electric mixer on low speed. Add margarine or butter, salt, and black pepper. Gradually beat in milk till light and fluffy. Set aside.

Meanwhile, for vegetable sauce, in a large skillet cook zucchini, summer squash, shallots or onions, garlic, and chili peppers in oil till tender. Stir in spaghetti sauce and beans; heat through. Keep warm.

When mashed potatoes are cool, add egg and stir till well combined. Spread half of potato mixture in a greased 9-inch pie plate. Spread with pesto. Top with remaining potato mixture and spread evenly over pesto.

Bake potato mixture, uncovered, in a 475° oven about 15 minutes or till slightly puffed and light brown on top. Let stand 5 minutes. Cut into four wedges.

To serve, place a pesto potato wedge on each serving plate. Spoon warm vegetable sauce over each wedge. Garnish with fresh basil, if desired. Makes 4 servings.

Nutrition facts per serving: 542 calories, 22 g total fat (20 g saturated fat), 56 mg cholesterol, 1074 mg sodium, 79 g carbohydrate, 7 g fiber, 17 g protein.
Daily Value: *36% vitamin A, 75% vitamin C, 10% calcium, 35% iron.*

BUTTERNUT SQUASH RISOTTO WITH PUMPKIN SEEDS

Heat Rating: Hotter

Want a milder rice dish? Try a milder pepper such as ancho or New Mexico chili peppers.

2 dried pasilla or chipotle chili peppers
1½ cups cubed peeled butternut or acorn squash
1 bunch green onions, sliced
2 cloves garlic, minced
2 tablespoons olive oil or cooking oil
1 cup Arborio or medium grain rice
3 cups vegetable or chicken broth
1 cup shredded fontina or Muenster cheese (4 ounces)
¼ cup grated Parmesan cheese
¼ cup pumpkin seeds, toasted

Cut chili peppers open and discard stems and seeds. Cut into small pieces. Place in a small mixing bowl and pour boiling water over peppers. Let stand for 45 to 60 minutes. Drain and chop.

Place squash and a small amount of water in a medium saucepan. Bring to boiling; reduce heat. Cover and simmer about 10 minutes or till just tender. Drain and set aside.

In a large saucepan cook green onions and garlic in oil till tender. Stir in rice. Cook and stir for 5 minutes.

Meanwhile, in another saucepan bring the broth to boiling; reduce heat and simmer. Slowly add *1 cup* of the broth to the rice mixture, stirring constantly. Continue to cook and stir till liquid is absorbed.

Add *1½ cups* more broth, *½ cup* at a time, stirring constantly till the broth has been absorbed. This should take about 15 minutes.

Stir in cooked squash, chili peppers, and the remaining broth. Cook and stir till rice is slightly creamy and just tender. Stir in fontina or Muenster cheese and Parmesan cheese. Sprinkle with pumpkin seeds. Makes 4 servings.

Nutrition facts per serving: 452 calories, 23 g total fat (8 g saturated fat), 38 mg cholesterol, 1053 mg sodium, 52 g carbohydrate, 3 g fiber, 16 g protein.
Daily Value: 67% vitamin A, 22% vitamin C, 23% calcium, 30% iron.

BLACK BEAN AND BOURBON CHILI

Heat rating: Hotter

Bourbon and black beans team up with dried chili peppers to give this chili an interesting flavor. To give it a nice, thick consistency, mash the cooked black beans slightly with a potato masher before serving.

2 cups dry black beans
8 cups water
3 dried chipotle chili peppers
3 dried pasilla or ancho chili peppers, seeded and chopped
1 medium green sweet pepper, chopped (¾ cup)
1 medium onion, chopped (½ cup)
4 cloves garlic, minced
1 tablespoon cooking oil
1 tablespoon ground cumin
2 teaspoons dried oregano, crushed
½ teaspoon salt
2 14½-ounce cans chopped tomatoes
3 cups vegetable broth or chicken broth
½ cup bourbon or water
Dairy sour cream (optional)
Chopped avocado (optional)

Rinse beans. In a large saucepan or Dutch oven combine beans and water. Bring to boiling; reduce heat. Simmer for 2 minutes. Remove from heat. Cover and let stand for 1 hour. (Or, skip boiling the water and soak beans overnight in a covered pan.) Drain and rinse the beans.

Cut chipotle and pasilla chili peppers open and discard stems and seeds. Chop into small pieces.

In the same large saucepan or Dutch oven cook sweet pepper, onion, and garlic in hot oil till tender. Stir in cumin, oregano, and salt. Cook and stir for 1 minute.

Add *undrained* tomatoes, beans, broth, bourbon or water, and chili peppers to saucepan or Dutch oven. Bring to boiling; reduce heat. Cover and simmer about 2 hours or till beans are tender. Mash beans slightly to thicken mixture.

To serve, ladle chili into individual bowls. Dollop with sour cream and top with avocado, if desired. Makes 6 to 8 servings.

Nutrition facts per serving: 356 calories, 10 g total fat (3 g saturated fat), 6 mg cholesterol, 901 mg sodium, 48 g carbohydrate, 5 g fiber, 15 g protein.
Daily Value: 28% vitamin A, 55% vitamin C, 11% calcium, 39% iron.

FRESH HERB POLENTA WITH TOMATO-VODKA SAUCE

Heat rating: Hotter

Try this full-flavored tomato and vodka sauce tossed with hot cooked pasta or spooned over grilled fish, too.

3 cups water
1 cup yellow cornmeal
1 cup cold water
1 teaspoon salt
¼ cup snipped fresh basil or oregano or 1 tablespoon dried basil or oregano, crushed
¼ cup finely shredded Parmesan cheese
    Tomato-Vodka Sauce (see recipe below)
    Fresh basil (optional)

In a medium saucepan bring *3 cups* water to boiling. In a medium mixing bowl stir together cornmeal, *1 cup* cold water, and salt. Slowly add cornmeal mixture to boiling water, stirring constantly. Cook and stir till mixture returns to boiling. Reduce heat to low. Cover and simmer for 15 minutes, stirring occasionally. Stir in basil or oregano.

Immediately transfer the hot cornmeal mixture to a greased 2-quart square baking dish. Cool for 1 hour. Cover with foil and chill several hours or overnight till firm.

To serve, bake polenta, covered, in a 350° oven for 25 to 30 minutes or till heated through. Sprinkle with Parmesan cheese. Let stand for 10 minutes before cutting. Serve with Tomato-Vodka Sauce. Garnish with fresh basil, if desired. Makes 6 servings.

Tomato-Vodka Sauce: In a medium saucepan cook ¼ cup chopped *onion* and 1 clove *garlic* in 2 teaspoons *olive oil or cooking oil* till tender. Stir in one 14½-ounce can diced or chopped undrained *tomatoes*, 3 tablespoons *tomato paste*, 2 tablespoons *vodka or water*, ½ teaspoon *sugar*, ¼ teaspoon *ground red pepper*, ¼ teaspoon *salt*, and ¼ teaspoon *ground black pepper*. Bring to boiling; reduce heat. Simmer, uncovered, for 15 to 20 minutes or till desired consistency. Stir in 2 tablespoons *whipping cream*. Cook and stir till heated through. Makes about 2 cups.

Nutrition facts per serving: 170 calories, 5 g total fat (1 g saturated fat), 10 mg cholesterol, 622 mg sodium, 24 g carbohydrate, 2 g fiber, 5 g protein.
Daily Value: 10% vitamin A, 24% vitamin C, 6% calcium, 11% iron.

SWEET AND HOT BARBECUE SAUCE

Heat rating: Hotter

The sweet comes from the brown sugar and the hot comes from the half dozen jalapeño chili peppers.

1 medium onion, chopped (½ cup)
6 jalapeño chili peppers, seeded and chopped
2 cloves garlic, minced
1 tablespoon cooking oil
2 cups catsup
¼ cup packed brown sugar
¼ cup white wine vinegar
¼ cup orange juice
3 tablespoons Worcestershire sauce
1 teaspoon dry mustard

In a large saucepan cook onion, chili peppers, and garlic in hot oil till onion is tender. Stir in catsup, brown sugar, vinegar, orange juice, Worcestershire sauce, and mustard.

Bring mixture to boiling; reduce heat. Simmer, uncovered, for 10 to 15 minutes or till desired consistency. Makes about 3 cups.

Nutrition facts per tablespoon: 42 calories, 1 g total fat (0 g saturated fat), 0 mg cholesterol, 289 mg sodium, 10 g carbohydrate, 1 g fiber, 1 g protein.
Daily Value: 2% vitamin A, 26% vitamin C, 0% calcium, 2% iron.

SPICY MARINARA SAUCE

Heat rating: Hot

If this isn't hot enough for you, then add 1 to 2 seeded and chopped serrano chili peppers.

½ cup chopped onion
4 fresh hot chili peppers such as jalapeño or serrano, seeded and chopped
2 tablespoons olive oil or cooking oil
2 14½-ounce cans chopped tomatoes
1 6-ounce can Italian-style tomato paste
¼ cup water
1 teaspoon sugar
1 teaspoon dried oregano, crushed
1 teaspoon dried basil, crushed
½ teaspoon dried thyme, crushed
1 bay leaf
½ teaspoon salt
¼ teaspoon ground black pepper
Hot cooked spaghetti or other pasta

In a large saucepan cook onion and chili peppers in hot oil till onion is tender, about 5 minutes. Stir in *undrained* tomatoes, tomato paste, water, sugar, oregano, basil, thyme, bay leaf, salt, and black pepper.

Bring mixture to boiling; reduce heat. Simmer, uncovered, for 10 minutes or till desired consistency, stirring occasionally.

For a smoother sauce, transfer mixture to a food processor bowl or blender container. Cover and process or blend till smooth. Serve over pasta. Makes about 4 cups.

Nutrition facts per cup: 169 calories, 8 g total fat (1 g saturated fat), 0 mg cholesterol, 993 mg sodium, 22 g carbohydrate, 2 g fiber, 4 g protein.
Daily Value: 32% vitamin A, 119% vitamin C, 8% calcium, 20% iron.

HORSERADISH CREAM SAUCE

Heat rating: Hot

Serve this versatile fluffy sauce with sliced cold meat, poultry, or salmon, or steamed vegetables. Or, double the amount of sauce and serve with a roast beef dinner.

2   to 3 tablespoons grated fresh
    horseradish or well-drained
    prepared horseradish
1   tablespoon mayonnaise or salad
    dressing
1   clove garlic, minced
½   teaspoon dry mustard
½   teaspoon vinegar
¼   teaspoon sugar
⅛   teaspoon salt
⅛   teaspoon ground black pepper
¼   cup whipping cream

In a medium mixing bowl stir together horseradish, mayonnaise or salad dressing, garlic, mustard, vinegar, sugar, salt, and black pepper.

In a small mixing bowl beat whipping cream with an electric mixer till soft peaks form. Fold into the horseradish mixture. Cover and chill at least 1 hour before serving. Makes 1 cup.

Nutrition facts per tablespoon: 21 calories, 2 g total fat (1 g saturated fat), 6 mg cholesterol, 23 mg sodium, 1 g carbohydrate, 0 g fiber, 0 g protein.
Daily Value: 1% vitamin A, 2% vitamin C, 0% calcium, 0% iron.

TOMATILLO-PUMPKIN SEED SALSA

Heat rating: Hot

A food processor makes quick work of this salsa. If you don't have one, chop the ingredients by hand and toss them together.

2   tomatillos
1   large tomato, cut up (1 cup)
1   medium poblano chili pepper, seeded
    and coarsely chopped
½   small onion, cut up
¼   cup snipped fresh cilantro
2   jalapeño chili peppers, halved
    and seeded
1   tablespoon lime juice
2   garlic
½   teaspoon salt
¼   cup pumpkin seeds or sliced almonds,
    toasted

Remove husks from tomatillos. Rinse and cut into quarters. In a food processor bowl combine tomatillos, tomato, poblano chili pepper, onion, cilantro, jalapeño chili peppers, lime juice, garlic, and salt.

Cover and process till coarsely chopped. Transfer to an airtight container. Stir in pumpkin seeds or almonds. Cover and let stand for 1 hour to blend flavors or refrigerate till serving time (up to 24 hours). For best flavor, serve at room temperature. Makes about 2½ cups.

Nutrition facts per tablespoon: 8 calories, 0 g total fat (0 g saturated fat), 0 mg cholesterol, 27 mg sodium, 1 g carbohydrate, 0 g fiber, 0 g protein.
Daily Value: 0% vitamin A, 7% vitamin C, 0% calcium, 1% iron.

Keep track of your daily nutrition needs by using the information we provide at the end of each recipe. We've analyzed the nutritional content of each recipe serving for you. When a recipe gives an ingredient substitution, we used the first choice in the analysis. If it makes a range of servings (such as 4 to 6), we used the smallest number. Ingredients listed as optional weren't included in the calculations.

METRIC COOKING HINTS

By making a few conversions, cooks in Australia, Canada, and the United Kingdom can use the recipes in Better Homes and Gardens® *Hot & Spicy* with confidence. The charts on this page provide a guide for converting measurements from the U.S. customary system, which is used throughout this book, to the imperial and metric systems. There also is a conversion table for oven temperatures to accommodate the differences in oven calibrations.

Volume and Weight: Americans traditionally use cup measures for liquid and solid ingredients. The chart (top right) shows the approximate imperial and metric equivalents. If you are accustomed to weighing solid ingredients, here are some helpful approximate equivalents.
- 1 cup butter, caster sugar, or rice = 8 ounces = about 250 grams
- 1 cup flour = 4 ounces = about 125 grams
- 1 cup icing sugar = 5 ounces = about 150 grams

Spoon measures are used for smaller amounts of ingredients. Although the size of the tablespoon varies slightly among countries, for practical purposes and for recipes in this book, a straight substitution is all that's necessary.

Measurements made using cups or spoons should always be level, unless stated otherwise.

Product Differences: Most of the ingredients called for in the recipes in this book are available in English-speaking countries. However, some are known by different names. Here are some common American ingredients and their possible counterparts:
- Sugar is granulated or caster sugar.
- Powdered sugar is icing sugar.
- All-purpose flour is plain household flour or white flour. When self-rising flour is used in place of all-purpose flour in a recipe that calls for leavening, omit the leavening agent (baking soda or baking powder) and salt.
- Light corn syrup is golden syrup.
- Cornstarch is cornflour.
- Baking soda is bicarbonate of soda.
- Vanilla is vanilla essence.
- Green, red or yellow sweet peppers are capsicums.
- Sultanas are golden raisins.

USEFUL EQUIVALENTS: U.S = AUST./BR.

⅛ teaspoon = 0.5 ml
¼ teaspoon = 1 ml
½ teaspoon = 2 ml
1 teaspoon = 5 ml
1 tablespoon = 1 tablespoon
¼ cup = 2 tablespoons = 2 fluid ounces = 60 ml
⅓ cup = ¼ cup = 3 fluid ounces = 90 ml
½ cup = ⅓ cup = 4 fluid ounces = 120 ml

⅔ cup = ½ cup = 5 fluid ounces = 150 ml
¾ cup = ⅔ cup = 6 fluid ounces = 180 ml
1 cup = ¾ cup = 8 fluid ounces = 240 ml
1¼ cups = 1 cup
2 cups = 1 pint
1 quart = 1 litre
½ inch =1.27 centimetres
1 inch = 2.54 centimetres

BAKING PAN SIZES

American	Metric
8x1½-inch round baking pan	20x4-centimetre cake tin
9x1½-inch round baking pan	23x3.5-centimetre cake tin
11x7x1½-inch baking pan	28x18x4-centimetre baking tin
13x9x2-inch baking pan	30x20x3-centimetre baking tin
2-quart rectangular baking dish	30x20x3-centimetre baking tin
15x10x2-inch baking pan	30x25x2-centimetre baking tin (Swiss roll tin)
9-inch pie plate	22x4- or 23x4-centimetre pie plate
7- or 8-inch springform pan	18- or 20-centimetre springform or loose-bottom cake tin
9x5x3-inch loaf pan	23x13x7-centimetre or 2-pound narrow loaf tin or paté tin
1½-quart casserole	1.5-litre casserole
2-quart casserole	2-litre casserole

OVEN TEMPERATURE EQUIVALENTS

Fahrenheit Setting	Celsius Setting*	Gas Setting
300°F	150°C	Gas Mark 2 (slow)
325°F	160°C	Gas Mark 3 (moderately slow)
350°F	180°C	Gas Mark 4 (moderate)
375°F	190°C	Gas Mark 5 (moderately hot)
400°F	200°C	Gas Mark 6 (hot)
425°F	220°C	Gas Mark 7
450°F	230°C	Gas Mark 8 (very hot)
Broil		Grill

*Electric and gas ovens may be calibrated using Celsius. However, increase the Celsius setting 10 to 20 degrees when cooking above 160°C with an electric oven. For convection or forced-air ovens (gas or electric), lower the temperature setting 10°C when cooking at all heat levels.